LIMITLESS
SOUL

LIMITLESS SOUL

ALEXANDRA TERREY

CLARK & MACKAY

Limitless Soul

© Alexandra Terrey 2024

All rights reserved. No part of this publication may be reproduced, stored in a retrieval system, or transmitted in any form or by any means, electronic, mechanical, photocopying, recording or otherwise, without the prior written permission of the author.

ISBN: 978-1-923289-21-5 (Paperback)

 A catalogue record for this book is available from the National Library of Australia

Cover Design: Alexandra Terrey and Clark & Mackay

Format and Typeset: Alexandra Terrey and Clark & Mackay

Published by Alexandra Terrey and Clark & Mackay

Proudly printed in Australia by Clark & Mackay

Table of Contents

Intro/Preface...9
Foreword...11
Why Conscious Leadership?..13
Chapter 1: Introduction...17
    Lead yourself..18
    1.1 Master yourself and others..18
    1.2 What are conscious living and conscious leadership?......19
    1.3 What is Conscious Leadership 6.0?..................................20
    1.4 The purpose of Conscious Leadership 6.0........................23
Chapter 2: The CEB Method...29
    A: Thinking...31
    B: Awareness and attitude..32
    How to create an impact with the CEB Method.....................33
    C—Cognitive level..35
    E—Emotional level...54
    B—Behavioural level...57
    What is conscious leadership 6.0 methodology all about?......60
    What is the importance of impact and leadership?.................62
    Why do we need leaders?..62
    Start with knowing and understanding yourself......................69
    Success principles..71
Chapter 3: CEB—3 Dimensions..77
    Critical thinking..78
    Quality of behaviours and thinking..79
    How to bring quality of behaviours to systems.......................80
    How to integrate high-quality behaviour into your day-to-day............80
    Quality of relationships and connections are more important than quantity...82

Chapter 4: Team Culture..83
    Attitudes..97
Chapter 5: Emotional Evolution...................................100
    Moving to a higher state of decision-making...................109
    Self-coaching—emotions...139
    Life with meaning quiz..141
    Emotional fitness...148
Chapter 6: Our Limitless Mind.....................................154
    The three brains..163
    Behaviours—connection and communication..................170
    A leader's roles 172
Chapter 7: Effective and Influential Communication........175
    How to communicate effectively?.....................................176
    Foundation of influence—rapport....................................177
    The impact of active listening..178
    Body language...179
    Calibration..180
    Physiology...182
    How do you establish and maintain rapport?...................183
    Effective Listening Skills...184
Chapter 8: Behaviours and Reprogramming Your Language........194
Chapter 9: Stress and Pressure......................................197
    Techniques for dealing with stress and pressure................199
    The cycle of thoughts and behaviours..............................202
    Core needs—our internal drivers......................................204
Chapter 10: Practical Rules for a Fulfilled Life.............210
    1. Make the decision..213
    2. Self-study..214
    3. Take a break..215
    4. Vision and goals..216

    5. Time..217
    6. No regrets; no fears...218
    7. Watch your thoughts..220
    8. Perseverance and faith...221
    9. Passion and liveliness...223
    10. Eat the frog..224
    11. What you want versus what you don't want................224
    12. Don't yell, don't complain, and don't harm.................225
    13. Make conscious decisions...226
Chapter 11: Judgement and Mindset Shift...............................**228**
    Microhabits—techniques for change..................................230
Chapter 12: The CEB Method in Practice..............................**235**
Resources, Inspirations, and a Thank You to My Teachers and Mentors.....239
Resources...240

Intro/Preface

Leadership is influence. Conscious living creates a limitless soul.

What do I mean by that? We are influencing each other every day. Our parents, our teachers, and our friends influence us, our thinking, and our emotions, and we are influencing them back. We are conditioning each other from childhood to adulthood. We create beliefs and paradigms for each other. Those we have around us usually dictate what we become or are influenced by. They basically become directors of our own lives.

Now, how great it would be if someone told me when I was fifteen years old that I could actually influence someone else's life forever? I believe that would be the most valuable piece of wisdom at that time.

When I was in high school, my parents went through a long divorce. I was a sixteen-year-old girl in puberty. Ah, this is probably the worst age for girls and mums, right? I wasn't getting enough attention from my parents because they had their own problems to solve. I was needy and probably very annoying at this age and really needed someone to care about me. I couldn't get it from my parents, and I thought I found a way to get them to pay attention. I skipped school often. I stopped studying. I slowly became the worst student in my class. I was very close to being kicked out, but I was wondering why this hadn't happened yet. I was creating another problem for my parents with the hope they would care about me, but they didn't even know. (I honestly think I was pretty terrible at that age; I'm so happy I am not my own child!)

One day, my teacher came to me with a warm smile and a caring tone in her voice and asked me if I was okay. Wow—she didn't blame me for taking the whole class down. She didn't put me down for my low performance. She just asked if I was okay. I wasn't prepared for that. I thought she would be angry. She caught me off guard. My words were stuck in my throat, and I couldn't say anything. Tears were pushing through my eyes so hard that I had to squeeze my face in a weird way and cover my eyes to not let anyone see I was crying. I felt like I wanted to scream and cry so loud, my chest felt tight, and I couldn't breathe, but still, I pretended I was fine. She said again, "Are you okay? I know you, Alex; this is not you. I know something more is happening. You don't need to tell me, but I would like to see you get back on track and show me that you can be the best again. I know you want to go to university, and I know you can do it. I know you can be the best. I believe in you. I will watch you for the next six months." I started to cry and couldn't stop. She was there for me, and she cared. I promised I would make it happen. And I did.

She was a true leader. She recognised that something more was going on than just me being silly or not capable. She came from love, caring, and understanding. She didn't kick me out, she didn't scream. She wasn't angry. She was warm and calm. She said, "I believe in you," and she changed my life forever. She was a true friend, leader, challenger, mentor, guide and supporter. All that a leader should be. She inspired me by setting up the challenge for six months. I totally changed and improved my grades. I was accepted and later finished my university degree.

She was there when I desperately needed someone. She was there when I quietly asked for help. She made me believe in myself for my whole life. I actually sent her a message a few months ago, after almost twenty-eight years of waiting, and told her, "Thank you for everything." It was very emotional, and I was truly in a deep, grateful expression of life.

I'm sharing this story because I would love to bring attention to how important it is to know we are all influencers. This is how strongly a few words or sentences from you or someone else can influence your life forever. Can you see how big an impact you already have in everyday life?

This program is based on the principle of a deeper understanding of yourself and your ability to change and understand what needs to be changed and improved first and then take this transformation to your team members and help them to grow and improve while facilitating a great culture with a high level of psychological safety.

Foreword

In life, we meet people who come into our lives and impact us in a profound and deep way—both emotionally and energetically. I was asked to read *Limitless Soul*, and the first few chapters had me so engrossed I found it hard to put the book down—the words were speaking to my heart and soul. I was experiencing so many light-bulb moments that acknowledged so many things I had been masking or hiding behind out of fear and not understanding why I was feeling the way I was.

Limitless Soul has unburdened those fears and helped me to transmute into an enlightened being who has found purpose and passion for the journey that lies ahead.

The frameworks have provided a structure for understanding and breaking down the fears that hold us back so that we can understand what motivates them and overcome them.

Limitless Soul is a journey back to purpose and passion. Thank you, my dear friend Alexandra, for shining your light and helping us all in our life's journey.

—**Mike Beach-Head**

Why Conscious Leadership is the Key to a Limitless Soul

In *Limitless Soul*, we start a journey that goes beyond the mechanics of running a business or leading a team. This is a journey inward—into the essence of who we are and how that reflects in every aspect of our leadership, relationships, and results.

Over the course of my twenty-year business career, I encountered countless challenges and witnessed the impact of leadership at every level. Some leaders inspired and elevated while others unknowingly crippled growth, both for themselves and those around them. But there was one particular experience with a past leader that struck me deeply. It shattered my trust in leaders and left me questioning my appetite to become a leader.

That experience, however, became one of the greatest catalysts for change. It drove me to ask:

- **What makes a leader truly impactful?**
- **Why do some people thrive and lead with ease while others struggle and burn out?**
- **Why do some leaders inspire and some discourage?**

I realised that the difference wasn't in external strategies or skills alone—it was in the level of **consciousness** a leader brought to their role. Leadership, at its core, is a reflection of our inner world. Until we address the subconscious beliefs, emotions, and identities that shape our actions, sustainable success remains elusive.

This understanding fuelled my passion for uncovering the secrets of conscious leadership and the undeniable connection between inner awareness and outer success. It became my mission not only to transform my life but to guide others—business owners, entrepreneurs, and visionaries—toward leading with **clarity, purpose, and alignment.**

The foundation of conscious leadership

The past ten years have been the most fulfilling of my career, not because of external accolades but because of the profound focus on **human potential and growth.** Along the way, I was honoured to be nominated as **Leadership**

Coach of the Year by the International Coaching Group (ICG) in 2021 and to receive their **Rising Star Award** in 2019.

But these achievements were not the goal—they were byproducts of a deeper truth I had come to embrace: **When we lead from a place of inner alignment, the outer world naturally follows.**

With a master's degree in economics and certifications as a **professional coach and executive coach, emotional intelligence trainer, pranic healer, and agility change manager,** I began to integrate diverse modalities into my work. This blending of perspectives allowed me to approach leadership through the lenses of **mind, body, energy, and spirit.**

I came to realise that leadership training could no longer be limited to intellectual knowledge or performance-driven systems. Real, lasting transformation requires addressing **the whole person—emotionally, mentally, energetically, and spiritually.**

When business owners and leaders step into their roles with heightened consciousness, they not only create financial success but also **reshape the culture** around them, fostering environments of creativity, innovation, and long-term growth.

This is why Limitless Soul exists—to show that true expansion, both in life and business, starts from within. There is no ceiling to what we can achieve when we align with our higher selves and lead from a state of **awareness and authenticity.**

The intersection of growth and purpose

The skills, wisdom, and experiences I've gathered aren't for self-promotion. I believe deeply that this work is meant to empower others to unlock their **intrinsic power**—to bridge the gap between **personal development and business success.**

When leaders operate with conscious awareness, they naturally **inspire and elevate those around them.** Their teams become more cohesive, decisions are made with greater clarity, and businesses thrive not just financially but as **forces for positive change.**

This is the essence of limitless leadership—**the ability to tap into inner potential and create sustainable, fulfilling success** from a place of alignment.

Why this journey matters

Motivated by a passion for human psychology, neuroscience, energy healing, meditation and leadership, I committed myself to lifelong learning. My studies at **The Coaching Institute, Enterprise Agility University, Tony Robbins Inner Circle and Joe Dispenza's courses** in various coaching disciplines gave me the tools to refine my practice.

But conscious leadership isn't just about skills or techniques. It transcends conventional models by embracing **presence, self-awareness, intuition, and the wisdom of the heart.**

Too often, we rely solely on intellect and logic to drive decisions, limiting our ability to see the **full picture.** By shifting our focus from the **mind to the heart,** we activate a deeper sense of truth. In doing so, we unlock our ability to navigate complexity with ease, fostering stronger connections and **more impactful leadership.**

This shift isn't abstract—it's practical. Leaders who embrace **self-awareness, higher consciousness, and emotional fitness** experience greater resilience, creativity, and adaptability. They no longer react to external pressures but lead with intention, transforming both their businesses and their lives. They are achieving exponential and sustainable growth in business and improvement in their life.

The energy of leadership

I emphasise the importance of **vibration (frequency), energy, and intention** because they shape the reality we experience. Leadership isn't just about managing people—it's about **creating energy fields** that uplift and inspire. When a leader vibrates at higher frequencies of **confidence, gratitude, love and clarity,** they naturally attract success and abundance.

Conscious leadership taps into this energy, enabling business owners to build **wealth, influence, and impact** in ways that feel fulfilling and aligned with their higher purpose.

An invitation to transformation

I invite you to explore this path with me—to discover how unlocking your inner potential as a leader or business owner can **reshape your life and business.**

Through practical insights and transformational coaching, *Limitless Soul* will guide you to lead from within, forging a new path of expansion, prosperity, and **limitless growth.**

Because when we elevate our consciousness, we don't just grow our businesses—we **transform our lives, communities, and the world around us.**

Let's take that first step together.

Chapter 1

Introduction

WHAT IS CONSCIOUS LEADERSHIP, AND HOW DO I DEFINE IT?

Conscious leadership goes beyond traditional leadership practices by emphasising daily conscious living, mindfulness, and presence. It is a transformative approach that integrates self-awareness, authenticity, connection with self and others on a deeper level of awareness, focus on communication, influence, understanding one's emotions, and a deep connection to the present moment.

For me, conscious leadership is about being fully present and engaged in every interaction, decision, and action. It entails cultivating a heightened sense of awareness, both internally and externally, to understand oneself, others, and the dynamics at play. It is almost like seeing beyond the form.

Conscious leadership involves living with intention and purpose, aligning one's actions and decisions with deeply held values and principles. It encourages leaders to regularly reflect on their own beliefs, biases, and limitations, fostering personal growth and self-evolution.

In the realm of daily conscious living, conscious leadership prompts individuals to bring mindfulness to their thoughts, emotions, and behaviours. It means being conscious of the impact of one's words and actions on others and actively seeking to create positive and inclusive environments.

Presence plays a pivotal role in conscious leadership. It is about showing up fully, listening deeply, and empathetically connecting with others. By being present for themselves and others, leaders can create safe spaces for open dialogue, encourage diverse perspectives, and build trusting relationships.

Ultimately, conscious leadership is an ongoing journey of self-discovery and growth. It invites leaders to continuously deepen their self-awareness, expand their consciousness, and embody their values in their leadership roles. By integrating daily conscious living and presence into their leadership approach, leaders can create meaningful and lasting impact within their teams and organisations. And more than that, they are able to help others on a deeper level.

Lead yourself

As I said before, we are all influencers and therefore we must take responsibility to understand who we are, what triggers us, how we think, what we feel, and how we behave. Our language and body language are expressions of ourselves and are what influence others. Our own goals, KPIs, or positions should not be used to motivate others. It's us—our mood, energy, internal balance, presence, authenticity, and emotional state. Yes, you read that correctly: our internal state and mood influence others and, as we know, our inner state dictates our outer world.

I love this topic. I hope I will be a great guide for you to show you how to know yourself better, master your inner world (and, therefore, outer world), recognise who we are and who others are, and learn to appreciate them for who they truly are while helping them to grow and master themselves too. Being authentic and present in every moment and situation without judgement and resistance is a mastery. To me, deep understanding is true leadership.

1.1 Master yourself and others

I was searching for a few years for the right books, reading, seeking, and searching for truth. I wasn't sure how to express what I felt—the experiences I went through as a person and as a leader and also collecting all of my experience through growth, action-implementation, and processes.

Based on reading, learning, implementing, and putting all of this through tests and processes, I was able to develop the Leadership 6.0 methodology that changed my way of looking at every person and every problem and also changed some of my clients' lives and moved us to a greater expression of ourselves, authenticity, inner peace, joy, and true high-performance leadership while creating psychological safety and wellbeing.

The Leadership 6.0 methodology is based on six elements we need to master to become unstoppable and impactful human beings. Let's start from the beginning.

1.2 What are conscious living and conscious leadership?

In a world that often sleepwalks through life, conscious living and leadership emerge as beacons of possibility. It's a realm I hold close to my heart, for it's my belief that as humans, we slip into a state of unconscious existence for the majority of our days. We become unwittingly programmed, almost robotic, after the age of thirty.

The shift towards consciousness is profound. It's about illuminating each moment and embracing it without the shackles of bias and judgement, or the turbulence of reactive emotions driven by our primal instincts.

Let's learn a little bit more …

A shift towards conscious living and conscious leadership. This paradigm speaks to me at the very core of my being, for I stand witness to a world that often traverses life's moments half-asleep, unaware of the richness that each breath holds.

As we journey through our days, we find ourselves entangled in the threads of societal conditioning. I can almost say we are living out scripts handed down by a world eager to define us. The question then arises, how do we awaken from this slumber?

Conscious living heralds the dawning of a new era. It beckons us to bring our attention to each passing moment, to bear witness to the unfolding of life before us. It is a state of being that transcends biases, judgments, and the tempestuous sea of emotions fuelled by our primal instincts. As we step away from the shadows of our amygdala's fight-or-flight response, we step into a realm of clarity, where wisdom and discernment reign. I was able to witness my clients' transformation in front of me when they moved away from the amygdala and left the ongoing stress mode for a few minutes towards clarity and their heart centre. They were able to find their true visions and the purpose of their lives in a few minutes. The realisation that we all have this inside of us, that we all have the power to connect with ourselves and access the wisdom of higher consciousness, was profound.

Sometimes, we are so disconnected from ourselves, so far away, conditioned by society and experience, that we can't find the path towards ourselves again. But trust me, it is possible.

I experienced that myself, and I witness this transformation with my clients on a daily basis.

In this luminous space, we discover the power to make decisions that resonate with the deepest chambers of our hearts. We unearth the ability to make choices that honour not only our individual paths but also the collective journey we share. Here, conflict finds resolution not through the bluster of force, but through the gentle caress of understanding and empathy.

Conscious leadership extends this transformative journey into the realm of influence and impact. It is the art of leading not from a place of authority but from a place of authenticity. A conscious leader is one who stands tall in the face of adversity, anchored in the knowledge that their strength lies not in the might of their position, but in the depth of their integrity.

In the realm of conscious leadership, innovation blossoms. A leader tuned into the present moment sees opportunities beyond the horizon. It fosters a culture of trust, where every voice and idea is valued.

To me, conscious living and conscious leadership are not mere aspirations but are attainable outcomes, beckoning us towards a future where we work not in the pursuit of busyness, but in the pursuit of purpose. It is a future where our actions reverberate with intention, where our decisions echo with the resonance of our shared humanity.

As we traverse this path, let us remember that conscious living and conscious leadership are not distant summits but are intimate companions on our journey towards a more meaningful existence.

1.3 What is Conscious Leadership 6.0?

In the realm of Leadership 6.0, we uncover a six-fold path towards achieving mental agility, flexibility, resilience, and vitality, and as a leader, we gain the ability to create a culture of kindness and a culture of high performance. This journey hinges on a profound fusion of neuroscience, emotional intelligence tools, behavioural science, values-driven frameworks, critical thinking models, and the art of mindful communication and deeper connections.

It's a fusion woven together by innovative quality metrics and benchmarks.

I hold a strong belief in the urgent need to bridge the chasm in traditional leadership education. It's time to elevate it to a realm where we not only understand the mechanics of human behaviour, thought, and emotion but also grasp how they shape the tapestry of our day-to-day life, culture, organisational health, and individual wellbeing.

Within this model lie six pivotal elements that leaders must not only comprehend but master:

1. Understanding yourself

Diving into your inner world, exploring both the shadows and the light, unravels thinking patterns, conditioning, and the filters through which your brain processes information. This self-awareness lays the foundation for identifying your strengths and areas for growth: your dark thoughts and emotions and your positive and light thoughts and emotions. Your reaction to situations, both great and not-that-great. This is the most important stage to take you through awareness and self-awareness and the courage to understand the simplicity of the present moment, mindfulness, and its massive impact on day-to-day operations, people, and culture.

2. Mastering your emotions

Becoming an emotionally adept leader opens doors to heightened mental agility, unlocking greater intelligence and sharpening decision-making. This emotional fitness provides the space to forge deeper connections and foster relationships that resonate. Emotional fitness is a journey that starts with understanding ourselves and embracing our vulnerabilities and our emotions, which can be darker, like fear, frustration, anger, or even shame, and also emotions like a high level of excitement, and finding the courage to be authentic and understand that making decisions from high or very low levels are not serving us and others. It's about learning how to create a state of ease and flow. It's about letting go of expectations and ego and, ultimately, discovering meaning and purpose in our lives.

3. The brain from a scientific lens

Unravelling the intricacies of the brain enhances critical thinking, reduces stress, amplifies mental agility, and sparks creativity and innovation. It enables you to discern which facets of your cognitive powerhouse are engaged in different scenarios and to engage both sides of the brain: the left brain and the right brain, masculine and feminine side, analytical and creative side. It shows you how living and acting from the amygdala leads us to automated living and how moving from the amygdala hijack towards heart-centred living and leading can take us to knowledge, wisdom, understanding, and inner joy. It demonstrates how removing ourselves from fight-or-flight mode helps us to unlock our subconscious patterns and move consciously to patterns that serve us.

4. The art of mindful communication

Profound insights into both overt and covert social dynamics, coupled with an understanding of how body language influences perception, pave the way for enhanced confidence and positive influence. When we're truly present, we can feel the rhythm of life, the pulse of existence. We can feel and sense each other and, from that space, it is so much easier to authentically communicate. There is no fear of conflict and doubts all are removed. Now, think about how this relates to communication. When we're truly listening, not just with our ears but with our whole being, we're sending a powerful message to the person speaking. We're saying, "You matter. Your words matter." This creates a space of trust and connection, like two streams converging into a river.

5. Mindful behaviours

Grasping your behavioural patterns, learning styles, energy dynamics, and sources of motivation empowers you to inspire others. It fosters an environment where individuals feel heard, seen, and valued, leading to heightened trust, collaboration, and engagement.

6. Mastering observations and measurements

Proficiency in utilising novel qualitative measurements for emotions, behaviours, and life domains, along with crafting criteria for evaluation, marks a shift towards a more refined level of performance. This entails implementing transformative shifts in thinking and behaviour and tracking progress to elevate the quality of interactions. Most importantly, this will help us to refocus from rigid measurements, such as KPIs, towards more qualitative measures and experiences. We are already able to measure a decrease in stress or exhaustion; imagine that you could start to observe how your life and relationships are getting better every day.

Our program is more than a theoretical exercise; it's an immersive experience, transformation designed for integration and sustainable growth and desired results. It is a lifestyle change and it is a connection to your higher self and wisdom within.

1.4 The purpose of Conscious Leadership 6.0

People don't need to be managed, they need to be unleashed.
—Richard Florida

Leadership is communicating to people their worth and potential so clearly that they come to see it in themselves.
—Stephen Covey

Once, my coach said, "Think about what you stand for; what is the most important to you, and what lifts your energy up in the coaching and leadership industry, or in your business and life?"

The answer was the Leadership 6.0 model. Why is that? What I love to do is look for gaps. I have run my businesses for nineteen years. How did I progress? I was closing the gaps. Every time I felt like my business was stagnating, I was looking for gaps and filling them to move forward and leverage more—leverage time, investment, or structures. Later, I realised a big part of this is better communication, deeper relationships, and emotional fitness.

My passion for leadership was natural and came from my experience and from an interest in people who were able to lead countries, the world, and the masses. I was always curious about what they were doing differently.

Trust me, it wasn't their managerial style or just resilience. It wasn't their time management or project management. It was behaviour, communication, and invisible language beyond words. It was confidence, true belief in their vision, and competency.

There I learnt leadership is the art of influence.

What excites me about leadership is transforming people's thinking and shifting perceptions about leadership, behaviours, and people, helping them to understand that "leadership" is not only self-management, people-management, time-management, organisation, prioritising, productivity, and resilience, but also a deeper understanding of themselves, people's behaviour, thinking, energies, drivers, motivators, and learning styles. Understanding ourselves and others and building up emotional fitness as a foundation for organisational health is the key to success.

Amazing leaders, such as Mahatma Gandhi, Mother Teresa, Nelson Mandela, and Martin Luther King Jr, demonstrated remarkable leadership virtues that inspired and transformed the world. While their approaches and contexts were different, they shared several common leadership virtues:

- **Compassion.** Both Mother Teresa and Mahatma Gandhi exemplified deep compassion for the suffering and marginalised. They dedicated their lives to serving others and championing the rights and dignity of all individuals, regardless of their social status, ethnicity, or religion.

- **Humility.** Despite their immense influence and recognition, these leaders remained humble and grounded. They viewed themselves as servants of the people and prioritised the needs of others above their own. Their humility allowed them to connect with people on a profound level and build genuine relationships.

- **Nonviolence.** Mahatma Gandhi is renowned for his philosophy and the practice of nonviolent resistance (*satyagraha*), while Mother Teresa advocated for peace and love in her actions. They both believed in the transformative power of peaceful resistance and nonviolent means to bring about social change, justice, and reconciliation.

- **Courage.** These leaders displayed immense courage in standing against injustice and challenging the status quo. Despite facing numerous obstacles and resistance, they fearlessly pursued their visions of a better world, inspiring millions to join their causes.

- **Persistence and resilience.** Mother Teresa and Mahatma Gandhi encountered significant challenges and setbacks throughout their journeys. However, they persevered with unwavering determination, resilience, and an unyielding belief in their missions. Their ability to stay committed in the face of adversity became a source of inspiration for others.

- **Authenticity.** These leaders were authentic in their words and actions, aligning their beliefs with their behaviour. They lived their values and principles, earning the trust and respect of those they led. Their authenticity made them relatable and accessible to people from all walks of life.

- **Visionary leadership.** Mother Teresa and Mahatma Gandhi had powerful visions for a more compassionate and just society. They communicated their visions effectively, inspiring others to join their movements and work towards a common goal. Their ability to rally people around a shared vision created a sense of purpose and unity.

I love Nelson Mandela's leadership and really admire him for his **forgiveness.** Mandela embodied the virtue of forgiveness, both personally and politically. Despite enduring twenty-seven years of imprisonment under the oppressive apartheid regime, Mandela advocated for reconciliation and forgiveness rather than seeking revenge. His ability to forgive and promote healing played a crucial role in the peaceful transition to democracy in South Africa. The **courage** Mandela displayed throughout his life is inspiring. He fearlessly stood against apartheid and fought for equality and justice. Despite facing immense personal risks and hardships, he remained steadfast in his convictions, inspiring others to join the struggle for freedom and equality.

Mandela's **leadership qualities** were characterised by his ability to inspire and unite people. He possessed a vision for a more inclusive and democratic South Africa, and his leadership style emphasised consultation, collaboration, and inclusivity. Mandela's leadership was rooted in empathy and a deep understanding of the diverse needs and aspirations of the South African people.

Mandela understood the importance of **patience** in achieving lasting change. He recognised that the struggle for freedom and justice required long-term commitment and perseverance. Mandela demonstrated patience in negotiations, working towards a peaceful transition to democracy and the dismantling of apartheid.

Most importantly to me, these are true leaders who are overcoming self-promotion and focusing on others and the greater good. True leadership starts with a journey to yourself. All those amazing leaders would not be able to demonstrate all those virtues without finding themselves, finding their true authentic passion, and understanding themselves on a deeper level. They move on the map of consciousness (Dr Hawkins) from fear, shame, guilt, and anger to courage, acceptance, and unconditional love. Those leaders are true conscious leaders.

These are all amazing qualities in human beings and yes, those make you a pretty great leader, but I truly believe there is more to it than this. There is a level of consciousness those people had, a level of mindfulness and courtesy.

They have inner drive and intentions guiding them from the space of a deeper understanding of life and the dynamics of relationships. It's deeper than you can imagine.

Why am I saying this?

I work with high-level executives and they all came to me at the point in their lives when they wanted something more than a powerful position or financial wealth. They wanted true success; they wanted achievement with fulfilment. They wanted to lead their lives and people more naturally, with an ease and alignment that feels like a flow or effortless living.

They came to me already successful at some level. They had built some level of financial wealth. Some of them were running or even sold some of their companies and were pretty rich. But there was something missing. There was something that made them sad, frustrated, or empty from time to time. They were not sure how to be happy or feel joy again. They thought they had it from time to time when they were with their families, but it was still a very transactional feeling, a very shallow feeling.

Some of them may experience anxiety, shallow breathing, burnout, demotivation and, sometimes, a kind of bitterness or maybe just very simple numbness.

When we start working together, I have a natural gift to see through and feel what is happening. I have some insights from my observations. In most people, there is a massive gap between their logical and emotional levels of experience.

They know and can explain or justify everything on a logical level. For example:

- I know I have to be more positive and I am pretty good with that.
- I know my ego is pushing me to compete with others from time to time, but I can see it and logically stop it.
- I know my values and am trying to live by them.
- I'm family-oriented—we spend every weekend together and things seem to be going okay; we have good relationships.
- I'm pretty good with people. I have enough clients and partners; we are doing well.
- I know I get triggered sometimes when I see someone better than me, but I have learnt to not react.
- Yes, some situations irritate, me but I am okay with it and can suppress emotional outbursts.
- I believe it's better to collaborate than compete.
- I like to help people.
- I know mindfulness and I meditate or pray daily (some visualise daily).
- Yes, I am exercising gratitude daily or weekly.
- We have a pretty good team; we have our social barbecues once a month and everyone is chill and friendly.

I have heard so many statements like these above, and while they are all true to some degree on a logical level, they are not true on an emotional level.

What do those statements mean on an emotional level? How they are disconnected?

- "I know I have to be positive and I am good at it" is a very logical comment. But mostly, when we look closer, people are not feeling very positive. Emotionally, they are feeling more dissatisfied than positive. That means that, at some level, it is pretending.
- "I know my ego is pushing me to compete with others from time to time but I can see it and logically stop it." This is true—we can bring awareness to our ego and logically catch ourselves and not respond to this trigger. But emotionally, we feel down—we doubt ourselves and

compare ourselves to others, and that inner feeling gets strong inside of us and causes anxiety or stress. Emotionally, we suppress it, but we don't work through it, so it gets stuck internally and causes illness inside of our body. I had a client who wanted deeper connections with people. He wanted to help people but, at the same time, while with me or others, he is telling himself, *But how I can do it? She's been doing this for longer; she is better than me*, and because of this deep emotion of impostor syndrome or self-doubt, he is keeping himself away from collaboration or fast growth and success. This is the same with the statement "I know it is better to collaborate than compete, especially in business." This is mostly on a personal level. Please remember, it is always nice to have some level of competitiveness—it helps us to grow. But when it starts to trigger emotions of self-doubt or lowering confidence, that's when it starts to create a self-sabotage pattern that holds you back. That means healthy competition is without extreme feelings about ourselves. It is more of an act or mindset of "I am going to make this happen" or "I am going to win." Not the mindset of "I am not good enough" or "she is better than me."

- "I know mindfulness and I meditate daily or pray daily." / "Yes, I am exercising gratitude daily or weekly." Those two statements can be true on a logical level and practical level. You may have discipline around this. Maybe it is your morning routine. But I can tell you right now you can give up if this is not done with a real emotional connection to the experience. If you practise your gratitude or journalling or praying on an intellectual level and it becomes just a routine or another thing to do, it's wrong. If you are truly feeling a deep emotion of love and a warm feeling in your body while doing it, that is the right way to do it. You need to change your emotional and energetic level while doing this practice so you can change your frequency and life.

- I like to help people. Check on yourself. Are you truly helping people every day without expecting anything back? Are you doing it when no-one is watching you? Are you truly doing it with the intention of helping someone become even better than you without being scared or bothered about it? That's the real feeling of service.

Chapter 2

The CEB Method

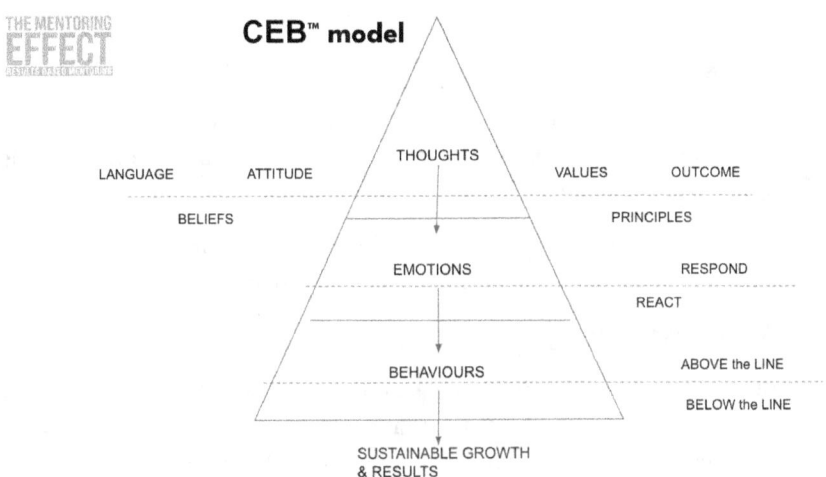

I'm fascinated by simplifying work for leaders and managers by reducing complexity and complication into simple criteria and steps. It is hard to measure the qualitative part of our life or team's performance without using KPIs or quantitative tools, but we can create criteria that will help us to understand how to measure and better understand our thinking, emotions, and behaviours.

Now, before I go on to explain those criteria, let's have a look at why I'm even trying and why I developed the CEB method.

Why? I was in leadership for the past eighteen years, and I was always asking myself these questions:

- What motivates and inspires me?
- What motivates people to perform better?
- Why should they do what I tell them to do?
- When do I feel like doing something without putting too much effort or feeling resistance?
- How do I remove resistance from my life and day-to-day routine?
- What if I don't tell them what to do?
- Would it be possible to keep them motivated or inspired and achieve goals without my involvement?
- What makes a leader an inspirational leader?
- What makes people or teams great, engaged, and collaborative?
- Why are two teams of the same size so different?
- Why is one team so easy to lead and comes to resolutions and solutions easily and the other is so challenging and never agrees on anything, almost like they don't like each other at all?
- What makes teams self-organised in a high-performing, sustainable way and, at the same time, innovative/responsive?
- What makes you a great leader?

I can write the whole book on questions I always have. While I was coaching for a US corporation, my major task was observing people's behaviour and performance. I was doing that for so long and helping people on the level of behaviour and performance that I realised we were going back to the same issues with some people. It was one cycle on and on with the same habitual behaviours that changed or improved for a few weeks or days and came back again like a boomerang.

I was trying to help people on the level of results and behaviour. I was supporting them on the action/execution level, on the **"how"** level. If you are scared of public speaking, prepare yourself, train, deliver, and I'll give you feedback. Repetition, repetition, and you will get better. But it didn't work for me. I put myself out there. I prepared for my speech, I repeated it thirty, sometimes fifty times before the speech itself and still, I felt stressed and insecure. It wasn't enough. Yes, repetition is the second most important part. To me, the most important part is the mindset. I mean mindset in a few different ways relating to the event and performance. It is the relationship with myself, the connection to myself, and the authenticity, and also the relation to the circumstances, emotional fitness, and level of consciousness.

But before this realisation, all that I was doing to myself and all the help I provided was on the level of execution. I wasn't aware of what was missing, but I knew *something* was missing.

I was telling people what to do differently, who to talk to, how to manage workload between team members, how to let people do the part of the work they are good at, how best to deliver, what to not forget, and what to focus on what to improve, but I didn't teach them how to think for themselves, how to feel good every moment, and how to add value to each other from their full presence and become more mindful. I was basically making them need me, and that was wrong. It was totally wrong from the perspective of what I truly wanted to achieve: transformation and a profound experience of life and trust.

Later on—maybe too late, upon reflection—I realised that I had totally disregarded that there is more to how we execute or do things. There is so much more in achieving sustainable results and sustainably great execution. Our results, actions, and behaviours are a direct reflection of our thinking and emotions. I didn't know that at that time.

This concept came to me after working with teams for years and after studying and reading all about psychology, neuroscience, behavioural science, coaching, and the foundations of different cultures and religions. I realised that we can all work hard and do the right things and never achieve the same results or outcomes when compared to someone else doing the same or less work with the right intentions, emotional and energetic alignment, and connection.

What's the difference?

Thinking and emotions! Experience and relation to ourselves and life!

A: Thinking

What we focus on is what we get. In simple words, the thoughts we focus on predominantly during the day are what results and circumstances we create, and that is how we feel. Our beliefs and mindset are creators and influencers.

Our limiting beliefs about ourselves or others or situations are limiting our results and experience.

What is really important at this level is our relation to our thoughts or focus on particular thoughts, our outlook on life and beliefs about life, beliefs about ourselves, our capabilities, and our identity, possibilities, and skills.

B: Awareness and attitude

What is our attitude towards our life, health, goals, and dreams? What is our attitude towards ourselves and others? What is our thinking or attitude when no-one is watching?

Do we just think about that big dream and do nothing because we believe it is too big for us? Maybe it's not realistic. Maybe we are scared and making excuses. What are your thoughts? Are you taking responsibility for your life and results?

Do you have big dreams or goals? I can tell you a secret! Nobody has the right to tell you that your dream is unrealistic, because they can't see what you see and they may have limiting beliefs about themselves and reflect that on you! That is their problem. You can do it, because you are more than capable of achieving whatever you want.

I didn't realise that people were limited by their beliefs, their thinking patterns, their past experiences, and any small moment in their life that may create bias or limits they are not aware of.

Once I looked deeper into why we didn't actively change to positive behaviours in a sustainable way, it became so clear. We didn't change our thinking. We didn't shift awareness and self-awareness. We didn't rise into conscious living.

I started to investigate what people think and believe.

What do high performers think, and what do low performers think? What is the difference? I realised there was more to this. I can create three major categories that need to be considered in our performance or the results we are getting—three categories that are influencing our own harmony, results, and success and also our team's success. Living consciously on these three levels allows us to change people's lives and impact them in a positive way just by being with them, just by sharing our space with them.

How to create an impact with the CEB Method

Notes from sessions with my clients

I have been working with John for the last four months. He is part-owner of a big communication company that is growing exponentially. They are opening up branches all around the world and Australia, and they are experiencing constant growth. But he doesn't see it that way.

Let me tell you what is going on in detail to give you a little bit of understanding of why this is so important. He sought coaching and mentoring because he wanted to become a better leader. He already had an idea he needed to start with himself and then help others in his team. He knows he is a pretty good leader, has a great ability to grow their business, and was always a very switched-on, smart, and driven person. Well, the results spoke for themselves. Company growth was massive every year—hiring new people, opening branches, and moving to bigger offices in Europe, Australia, and now the US.

We started with some basic sessions about what was going on in his life and how he runs the company, and I was listening to how he thinks about people and himself. At first, I noticed he couldn't sit still. When he was sitting on the couch at home watching the kids, after a few minutes, he would stand up and need to do something. When he is on holiday, he sits for five minutes at the pool and needs to stand up and go for a walk or run or do something. On his days off, he always checks his email and is always involved in business. He is there for people all the time. People seek him for answers and advice. People in his team check with him when they need to make big or small decisions. He felt that this was great leadership because his door was always open and people would come to see him daily. But he was mistaken.

He was always unhappy that his business partner was micromanaging, was too involved in unnecessary tasks, was slow in decision-making and was not seeing the big picture or thinking ahead. John was amazing at forward-thinking—don't get me wrong, he was a master at his job. But he wasn't mastering his internal world and didn't have any idea that, by doing more, he was disempowering his team.

Now, after three months, I suggested doing values elicitation in a different way. I used a lot of different questions and also utilised the DeMartini method and, funnily enough, we actually didn't elicit values, as such, but we found a lot of thinking, emotional, and behavioural patterns that started to make a lot of sense. It brought to light a reason why he was always running and chasing—why he always felt like everyone around him was too slow.

I asked him about his life and work in different ways. I asked him what his passion was, how he spent his money, how he liked to spend his time, what he kept, what he liked to converse about, read about, and who he liked to have around, and so on. There was a common thread in his answers, and it struck me when he said he doesn't keep trophies from all the competitions he has done. He doesn't care about new clothes or any material things that much, but still he wants to grow more and achieve more. There was no clear understanding of why. But this was when I saw the pattern: there is a limiting belief—there is this cognitive pattern that holds him to his standards and causes him to run.

I realised that this thought, sentence, and belief is keeping him "on the run" all his life without even knowing that he is constantly running away from himself.

When I got deeper and asked him a few other questions, he mentioned he grew up in a pub; that is to say, he and his parents lived above a hotel and spent much of their time drinking there with friends and family. I didn't need to know more. It was so clear that one of his major drivers was "I don't want to end up like this." His driver was fear; his driver was avoiding something that he thought might happen without realising how far away he was from that happening and without realising that he was not that person.

This premise was keeping him away from real growth and from evolution. He stayed stuck emotionally at that age when he saw himself in the pub looking at other people thinking, *I don't want to be like that.* That is where his emotional evolution stayed stuck with the premise that was driving his life.

We uncovered thinking patterns (limiting premise—thought) connected to emotional patterns (fear) that created behavioural patterns of never resting, never settling, and always running, which led to exhaustion and near-burnout.

He believed that "movement is growth" but, when we looked back on the previous month, he realised the most growth he'd had was when he took a step back from business and day-to-day and reflected and paused. We reframed the whole idea of movement to include actually pausing and seeing. Ongoing movement and running are blindness and inflexibility. It is actually the opposite of what we believe.

Pausing and sometimes feeling like going back is actually a gift that helps you to see things that you couldn't see. He realised that, and he transformed his life and the way he ran his business.

He stopped being the one who needed to advise all the time and help people make decisions. Instead of dictating and saying what needs to be done on projects, he asked his team members, "What do you think we should do? How would you do it if I were not here?" and told them, "You know the answers; I'm happy for you to try it."

He started to delegate more and understand that more free time has made him become a better leader. The ripple effect of his change was a massive transformation for all teams. He finally felt like he was empowering his team without trying to be involved all the time. By giving them more responsibility, he made them think for themselves. He didn't need a massive budget for his team training; all he needed to do was change the small nuances of his language and explore who he was internally and what was holding him back from being an authentic, conscious leader.

C—Cognitive level

This category consists of three major areas:

- **Why we think the way we do**—beliefs, values, goals/purpose
- **What our thinking patterns are**—experience, memories, language
- **How we think**—moving away from fear, resistance, and shame and moving towards courage, compassion, acceptance, understanding, and love to the highest level of unconditional love or enlightenment

Beliefs

Why do we think the way we think? This involves exploring the program that is driving our life decisions and choices.

This area is the most important to understand if you truly want to become an influential human being and inspiring leader. The reason we are all different—we act differently, we feel differently, and we respond differently in particular situations—is our belief system. Our belief system is formed from when we were born. How we were raised from birth to seven years of age is the most important period of the meaning creation or belief creation stage. What we observe in our environment from our parents, teachers, and people around us at that age helps to create a program that is almost like a photocopy of our parents', teachers', or friends' way of thinking and acting. So, we basically created a blueprint for our lives in our past, and we are still using this same blueprint for decisions and likes or dislikes when we are in our forties or fifties without realising it. We are programmed and we are, most of the time, not aware of that program, so we don't know what belief system creates our experience of life. We experience the world as *we* are, not as the world is. So, we are looking at this world through our own lens.

Beliefs are formed from the first day of our life. Even small things, like not getting attention and a hug from your parents when you were crying as a baby, form beliefs like "I am not enough" or "I am not lovable" or lead you to have lower self-esteem. Yes, crazy! Such a tiny moment in your life can set you up on a journey of less confidence, which will influence your choices, your study field, or career choices. One moment in your childhood and you allow it to define you. The good news is that, if you are reading this book, you know you can change everything because it is in your POWER. It's your decision to change how you feel about yourself. We are not here to blame parents; we are not here to become victims and find excuses for our behaviours. No! Definitely a big NO to this.

We are here to raise awareness, self-awareness, and the courage to change all our old patterns that don't serve us! Your old, unresourceful patterns or beliefs are not you! They don't need to define you. You can choose who you are becoming and who you are from this moment.

Ephemeral moments don't need to define your life, success, or relationships. Please remember the most important thing: you must be aware of your thinking or emotional patterns and your limiting beliefs, and then you can break them and become unstoppable. It is your self-awareness, self-reflection, and coaching that can uncover all those limits, and you have all the power to shift these around. This work can be done in a very short time when you find the right guide, coach, or mentor to help you dig deeper, find those deep inner limitations and inner blockages in your nervous system, and help you reinvent yourself.

Back to beliefs. Based on your belief system, you create your internal representation of the world. Your opinion. Your way of seeing things. Your perspective. Your glasses or the lens you see the world through.

You can change your lenses anytime and pretty quickly, the same way as with a camera.

Beliefs are what we think is true about ourselves, our colleagues, our team, our organisation, the market, people, and life in general. Beliefs are what we believe about our brand, product, and service. If we don't believe our product is adding value to people's lives or providing a solution we promise, we won't be able to sell it.

For example, people think that when they are employees, they work for someone. The biggest mistake is to believe you are working for someone else.

Remember, you are working for yourself, for your future, for your improvement, for your life experience, for whatever reason and passion you have, for fulfilment and for the quality of your life and lifestyle you want. It doesn't matter who your employer is. I see so many entrepreneurs think they are free and have a different mindset and that they are better than employees, but the truth is, so many entrepreneurs just find themselves a job. The only difference is that they are their own boss. I found this even worse because they are the worst to themselves. They don't acknowledge themselves and they don't give themselves bonuses or days off, right?

If that's you, better to find a new employer—someone who will take care of you. It's not about the position or being an entrepreneur. Success in any area is about your level of thinking, emotions, and behaviours. It is about who you are and what you are embodying. Who are you? What are you? Are you a true entrepreneur, focusing on vision and growing something that will serve others? Do you understand that, as an entrepreneur, you have a responsibility to make it bigger and make your idea come true? As a leader, you have to have an entrepreneurial mindset and emotional state. You must understand that, as a leader, you look beyond. You don't get into day-to-day busyness and problems, you look for long-term higher solutions and take care of people who are working hard to make this vision a reality.

My biggest breakthrough that changed my business results and success in one month.

In the story of my business journey, there's a moment that stands out, a moment when everything changed. I remember it like it was yesterday. I was perched on a high day bed in the lounge room with a balcony view, legs hanging over, looking out at the stunning Balinese rice fields. The sound of water trickling into a nearby pool was like a calming and soothing melody. It was a quiet and beautiful place, a space where open-hearted conversations flowed naturally.

It was in this sacred space, amidst the memories and experiences of my life, that the greatest revelation of all emerged. I found myself attempting to articulate the struggle of fitting in, a theme that had occupied my journey for far too long. And then, in a moment that felt like the universe had whispered its wisdom, my coach gently posed a question that would alter the course of my professional existence: "Why are you trying to fit in?"

In that instant, the ground beneath me seemed to shift. The truth resonated like a bell tolling in the depths of my being.

"I don't need to fit in; I can stand out!"

The liberation that washed over me was like a heady elixir of freedom and empowerment. It was a seismic shift, a declaration of independence for my life and business.

With this new-found perspective, I embarked on a journey to run my business my way, unapologetically and uniquely. It was unconventional, a departure from the well-trodden path. I stopped pretending to be an entrepreneur and stopped giving myself jobs. I changed my mindset, but not only that, I changed the whole frequency I was operating from. Energy shifted. This decision rippled through every facet of our operations. Marketing and sales were no longer about chasing but about **magnetising and attracting those who resonated with our vision.**

For the first time in nineteen years of steering five different businesses, I felt a profound sense of freedom and unadulterated joy. This was not just a breakthrough, it was a liberation, a reclamation of my authentic voice in the realm of business. It marked a turning point not only in my professional journey but in the very essence of who I am and how I show up in the world.

This revelation has since become the cornerstone of my approach, a guiding light that infuses every decision and every interaction. It is a reminder that true success lies in authenticity, in standing out, and in embracing the unique essence that each of us brings to the world. As I carry this lesson forward, I do so with a profound sense of gratitude for the moment that set it all in motion, a moment in the embrace of nature's beauty and the sanctuary of open-hearted conversation.

At that moment, I realised more limiting beliefs than I was able to even comprehend at that time.

I realised that we are all very similar, and when I looked at my clients the week after this realisation, I saw similarities in beliefs and thinking patterns:

- Some people tried to fit in and, from childhood, they were plagued by expectations of others or their perceptions of what others expect them to be.
- Some people worked so hard and were so busy they lost track of who they were and totally disconnected from themselves.
- Some people believe they need to work harder, even during their weekends or holidays.
- Some of my clients believe working hard is the only way to wealth.
- Some of my clients believed there was not enough money, it was hard to make more, or that being successful meant a broken marriage or bad relationships with their kids.
- Some people on my client's team believed that, after a certain time, it was "overtime" and wouldn't do it unless paid for every minute.
- Some people believe that a great day is completing what's started and won't leave until it's done.
- Some people believe that the only way to succeed is to step on other people.
- Some people believe that the only way to succeed is with and through other great people.
- Some people believe that a great day is one of collaboration and talking rather than delivering.
- Some people believe there is not enough time or it's too late to start over again.
- Some people believe there is growth and progress when they do something and can't rest. When they stop, they think they are not growing. They are very restless … and the truth is, the biggest progress and growth is in stillness.

And we can go on and on and on. There are so many beliefs that are not serving us and are dragging our lives even further from ourselves without realising it.

I can give you a few examples of great beliefs especially if you are a leader leading a team that needs beliefs checked.

Beliefs that tend to get great results and build a great culture that attracts the best people:

- I'm enough.
- I'm present and listening openly.
- I learn the most when I'm quiet.
- I'm a servant leader and I'm here to support people and help them to grow.
- We are influencing each other emotionally and energetically.
- Emotional fitness is important, and we can check on each other every day.
- We can make it happen together.
- It's better working with people than against people.
- We are all important in this team and we are complementing each other.
- There's always a way.
- If it's going to happen, it's up to me.
- I am responsible for this, and I am taking full ownership of success or failure.
- You can count on me.
- I have my back and I trust myself and my team.
- When the going gets tough, I turn up ready to get it sorted.
- I am safe and I can express my concerns and give feedback.
- Feedback is a gift, and it is a great way to grow.
- When the going gets tough, I have to set the example of excellence for everyone.

- I am here to be the best I can be.
- I'm grateful.
- No-one makes me have a bad day—I do that all on my own.
- No other person has power over me and can't make me feel angry or frustrated. It is me doing that to myself.
- Happiness is a decision. I can decide how I will feel today and how can I enrich people's lives.

In the realm of personal development, one term that often takes centre stage is "limiting beliefs." These are the thoughts and convictions that subtly shape the way we perceive ourselves and the world around us. But where do they come from, and how do they weave themselves into the fabric of our reality?

A key player in this game is neuro-linguistic programming (NLP), a psychological approach that delves into the patterns of our thoughts and behaviours. NLP acts like a behind-the-scenes director, influencing the scripts we write for ourselves. It's through NLP that certain ideas, often adopted in our formative years, become the silent architects of our belief system.

At the heart of this process is our "sour filter," a term coined to represent the lens through which we perceive the world. This filter is shaped by a multitude of factors—upbringing, societal influences, memories, values, past experiences—and it tints our view of reality. It's like wearing sunglasses; they alter the way we see things, sometimes casting shadows where there are none.

These limiting beliefs, often born from NLP and nurtured by our sour filter, become the silent influencers of our choices, actions, and ultimately, our reality. They are the scripts that run in the background, shaping our responses to challenges and opportunities alike. They might sound like "I'm not good enough," "I'll never succeed," or "I'm destined to fail."

But here's the transformative truth: once we recognise these beliefs for what they are—mere scripts, not immutable truths—we gain the power to rewrite them. It's like being the author of our own story, able to edit and revise as we see fit. Through conscious awareness and intentional rewiring, we can dismantle the barriers that have held us back. But we can only do it and uncover those when we are brutally honest with ourselves. Put your ego aside and truly think, do you feel confident, or is there any small trigger, thought, or doubt that occupies your mind from time to time?

This process isn't about denying challenges or living in a state of perpetual positivity. It's about reclaiming agency over our narrative, acknowledging that we have the power to shape our reality and we are causing and creating our emotions. It's about recognising that, while we may not have control over external circumstances, we do have control over how we interpret and respond to them. And more than that, when we start changing our thinking and emotional patterns, our energy and frequency change and so do our circumstances and external environment.

So, as we navigate this journey of self-discovery and growth, let's remember that our perception is not set in stone. It's a canvas, waiting for us to pick up the brush and paint our own masterpiece. Through the alchemy of awareness and intention, visualisation and meditation, we can transform limiting beliefs into liberating truths, and in doing so, rewrite the script of our lives.

I don't agree that NLP should be everywhere as free training for coaches and consultants who want to use it on others, or as a short training such as a weekend course, or free from any regulations. If you want to do NLP, I would suggest studying it for your own transformation first without trying it on others. I believe NLP in the wrong hands can be a very dangerous tool. Also, I believe that, even if some great coaches have good intentions, it won't necessarily go well. I experienced a healing and transformational session with one of the coaches from the school where we studied together for a few years. It didn't go well and I had to look for alternative methods to help myself after this session.

I believe you need to master it and practise it for a few years before you take it to the public and offer it as one of your services. It can become a very dangerous, manipulative tool if not used the right way.

I never go back to using only this technique or use it as a whole process for one session. I believe it is great knowledge to have, to understand language and its influence on our emotions and behaviours. I found that part the most important in my coaching and mentoring. I use it as an observational and questioning tool to understand the client's map and limits.

Neuro-linguistic programming, in short, is a field of psychology that studies the language of the brain. Just a little explanation from my side.

The NLP model of communication—unlocking the mind to become limitless

Understanding the fundamentals of **neuro-linguistic programming (NLP)** is not just about becoming a better writer or communicator—it's about unlocking the subconscious patterns that shape your reality. When we learn how the brain filters and processes information, we gain the power to shift perspectives, dismantle limiting beliefs, and consciously create the outcomes we desire. This is a vital step on the journey to becoming limitless.

The way we interpret the world is rarely objective. Every experience, conversation, or event we encounter is processed through an intricate web of subconscious filters. These filters are shaped by our past experiences, values, attitudes, and deeply held beliefs—most of which operate beneath our conscious awareness.

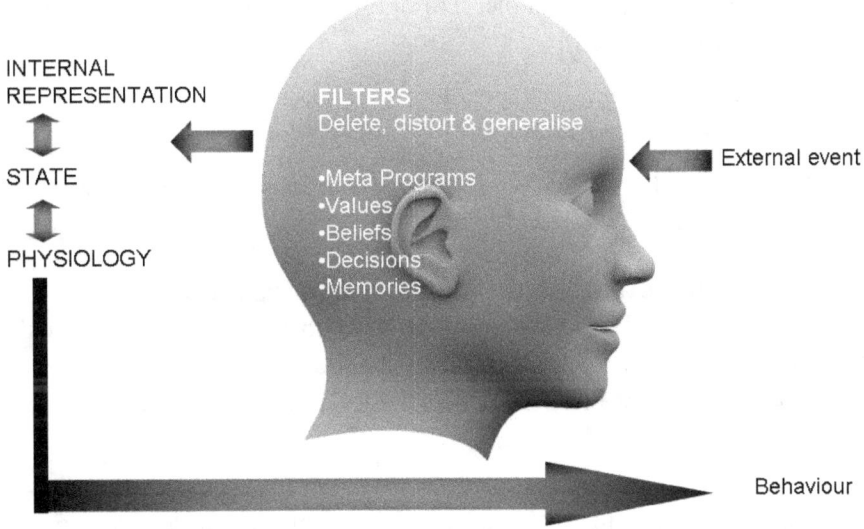

The model works like this:

An external event occurs—whether it's reading a piece of information, interacting with someone, or witnessing a situation—and the brain filters it through various lenses:

- **Values**—What matters most to us, often shaped by upbringing and life experiences.

- **Attitudes**—The mental and emotional stance we hold toward different subjects.
- **Beliefs**—Core convictions about ourselves, others, and the world.
- **Decisions**—Past choices that have reinforced certain thought patterns.
- **Memory**—Stored experiences that colour our present-day reactions.
- **Emotions**—Unresolved emotional experiences that linger and influence perception.
- **Language**—The words and internal dialogue we use to describe our reality.

This filtering process determines how we perceive, respond, and ultimately **store** information in our brains. The outcome can take one of three forms:

- **Generalised**—The brain applies broad assumptions based on limited experiences (for example, "I'm not good at public speaking" after one negative incident).
- **Deleted**—Important details are ignored or suppressed to fit a preconceived narrative.
- **Distorted**—Reality is skewed by emotions or beliefs, altering how events are remembered or interpreted.

Why is this important on the path to becoming limitless?

Because the subconscious mind governs up to **95%** of our daily actions and decisions. If left unchecked, these filters dictate how we see the world, what opportunities we recognise, and the level of success we believe we can achieve.

The difference between feeling stuck and experiencing breakthrough moments lies in our ability to **reprogram these filters consciously.** When we recognise how limiting beliefs and past experiences shape our reactions, we can begin to challenge those narratives and replace them with empowering ones.

Limiting beliefs hunting

Now, let's try a short exercise to unlock or uncover some of your inner limitations and limiting beliefs. Please use the following questions below and send me an email or a message back to share what you find out or what you learn about yourself.

1. Identify any limiting beliefs

Take your desire and insert your answer into the sentences below, which will help you identify any limiting beliefs.

- I want to have _____, but _____. (for example, "I want to be a great-looking woman and lose 5 kg, but I have a family and don't have time to cook special meals for myself.")
- The reason I don't have _____ is because _____.

2. Exploring your beliefs

Limiting beliefs often hide beneath the surface, quietly shaping our decisions, actions, and ultimately, our results. The moment we take time to sit down, reflect, and honestly answer the deeper questions we avoid, these beliefs start to reveal themselves. They show up not just in our thoughts but in the patterns and outcomes we experience in life.

Look closely at the key areas of your life—**health, relationships, career, business, and finances.** If you find yourself consistently achieving the same results, feeling stuck, or repeating familiar cycles, it's a clear indicator that limiting beliefs are at play.

Our results are direct reflections of the beliefs we hold. By recognising this connection, we gain the power to shift those beliefs and open the door to new possibilities.

Let's dive into our first very important self-reflection exercise. Keep writing, journalling whatever comes to your mind. Reflect on the following questions:

- Do you know what success is? What does that mean to you?
- What does success truly mean to you, beyond societal expectations or external validations?
- How do you perceive yourself at your core? What boundless potential do you believe lies within you?
- What beliefs do you hold about the inherent potential and goodness in others?

- When you envision what's possible in your life, without limitations, what does that look like?
- How straightforward do you believe it is to manifest the outcomes and achievements you desire?
- What do you anticipate will unfold in your journey, based on your current beliefs?
- What values do you hold as deeply significant and guiding principles in your life?
- How do you perceive time, and how does this belief influence your actions and decisions?
- How does the thought about time make you feel?
- What do you believe about yourself, your identity, your possibilities?
- What do you believe about others?
- What do you believe is possible?
- What do you believe about how easy it is to create the results you want?
- What do you believe about time?

3. Unearthing limiting beliefs

- Is the belief you hold about a certain aspect absolutely true, without any room for doubt or exceptions?
- Can you genuinely, with absolute certainty, know that this belief is an unchanging reality?
- When you operate under the influence of this belief, what emotions arise? How do these emotions and feelings shape your actions and reactions?
- If you were to release this belief, who would you become? How would your actions differ?

4. Further exploring limiting beliefs

- When did you first adopt this belief as your own, and what circumstances led to its adoption?
- Can you imagine a reality where this belief doesn't hold true? Is it conceivable that this belief is merely a construct of your mind?
- How often does this belief genuinely align with reality? Can you recall instances where it didn't hold?
- What empowering belief would you prefer to adopt in place of this limiting one?
- How would your actions and decisions shift if you operated from the perspective of this new, empowering belief?

Universal beliefs—nominalisations

State what your global beliefs are about any nominalisation that you want clarity on. Nominalisations are concepts you can't really measure, such as love, relationships, and more.

Be brutally honest. Don't try to manipulate your answer or make yourself sound good. What are your conclusions, beliefs, and assumptions about the following nominalisations?

- Men are _____
- Women are _____
- Life is _____
- My body is _____
- Relationships are _____
- Health is _____
- A career is _____

I am sure you know people who always say something like "Life is hard" or "Why is my life such bad luck?"

Life is ... a journey? A game? A battle? An adventure? A mystery? A joy? Remember, you can think and believe whatever you want about life, but remember that what you believe is what you create and what you project!

- What is the metaphor(s) that you use to describe your life?

_____

_____

Those metaphors say a lot about our attitude towards life and our beliefs.

Identity beliefs

Our identity beliefs are an accumulation of historical data points. They are formed by the words "I" and "Am". I am ...

State what your identity beliefs are about yourself.

- I am _____

Fill in the blank ... a leader? A parent? Smart? Dumb? Attractive? Ugly? Fat? Skinny? Skilful? Knowledgeable? Capable?

Get radically honest. Don't try to manipulate your answer or make yourself sound good.

Choose the beliefs you need to shift that will serve you to achieve your goals and desired outcome.

Now, when you finish your exercise, I would like to know what your experience was. What was your biggest "aha" moment from this exercise?

You just experienced part of the coaching where we try to uncover what is truly happening in your life—what thought patterns are holding you back. I'm sure some of them came out. Please let me know.

The best way to break free from those limitations is to get a coach or just start slowly and be aware of those during your next few days. Catch yourself when you think the old way and try to consciously replace your beliefs in action.

Let's dive deeper into another concept filter that plays a big role in how we live our lives and what we achieve in our lives.

Values

Our perception is also based on our **values.** I will dive deeper into values in the later chapters, but for now, remember that our values are our emotional compass. We think through values, we make decisions based on values, and we create perceptions based on values.

Values are deeply held beliefs or principles that guide our thoughts, attitudes, behaviours, and choices. They serve as a compass, influencing our perceptions, motivations, and priorities in life. Values reflect what we consider important, meaningful, and desirable. They shape our identity, inform our decisions, and provide a framework for ethical judgments.

Values can be both individual and collective. Individual values are unique to each person and may be influenced by personal experiences, beliefs, and aspirations. Collective values, on the other hand, are shared by a group or society, reflecting cultural norms, traditions, and social expectations.

While values provide a moral and emotional compass, it is important to recognise that they can differ among individuals and cultures. What one person considers a core value may not hold the same significance for another. Additionally, values can evolve and change over time as we gain new experiences, knowledge, and perspectives.

Living in accordance with our values brings a sense of purpose, fulfilment, and authenticity. That's why awareness and understanding values are so important. When our actions align with our values, we experience greater congruence, integrity, and overall wellbeing. Conversely, when our actions contradict our values, we may feel a sense of internal conflict, dissatisfaction, or dissonance.

To me, the importance of the role of beliefs and values is in shaping one's motivation, resilience, and approach to challenges. We can distinguish between a fixed mindset (the belief that abilities are fixed and unchangeable) and a growth mindset (the belief that abilities can be developed through effort and learning). Values play a significant role in shaping individuals' mindsets and their willingness to embrace challenges and pursue growth.

Various authors and researchers have explored the question of whether we are born with values or not. One perspective is that humans have innate predispositions or tendencies that can influence the formation of values. However, it is important to note that this viewpoint does not suggest that specific values are predetermined or fixed from birth. Rather, it suggests that certain foundational capacities or tendencies may shape our capacity for moral development.

For example, psychologists such as Lawrence Kohlberg and Carol Gilligan have studied moral development and proposed that humans have an innate capacity for moral reasoning. They suggest that, as we mature, our moral values and understanding of right and wrong develop through stages of moral reasoning, influenced by both innate factors and social experiences.

On the other hand, other authors and researchers argue that values are primarily acquired through socialisation and cultural influences. They suggest that values are learnt and shaped through interactions with caregivers, peers, societal norms, and cultural practices. From this perspective, values are seen as products of our upbringing and social environment rather than innate qualities.

It is essential to consider that the nature versus nurture debate regarding values is complex and multifaceted. Most experts agree that both innate predispositions and external influences interact to shape our values. While we may have certain inherent capacities, the specific values we hold are primarily influenced by our interactions with the world around us and our conscious reflections and choices.

While the specific values individuals prioritise may vary, here are some commonly recognised values that can contribute to personal growth, positive relationships, and conscious living:

Integrity. Acting with integrity means being honest, trustworthy, and maintaining strong moral principles. It involves consistency between one's words, actions, and beliefs. And it only counts when you live it and breathe it even when no-one is watching.

Respect. Demonstrating respect involves treating others with dignity, fairness, and consideration. It involves valuing diverse perspectives and honouring the autonomy and worth of every individual. Respect, in simple words, is no judgement, more acceptance, and making an effort to understand others.

Compassion. Cultivating compassion entails showing kindness, empathy, and understanding towards others. It involves a genuine concern for the wellbeing and alleviation of suffering in oneself and others. It means you can walk in someone else's shoes and demonstrate deep empathy and understanding.

Responsibility. Taking responsibility means being accountable for one's actions and choices and their consequences. It involves fulfilling obligations, honouring commitments, and taking ownership of one's role in relationships and communities.

Courage. Embracing courage means facing challenges, adversity, and uncertainty with bravery and determination. It involves taking risks, standing up for what is right, and pursuing personal growth despite fears or obstacles.

Gratitude. Practising gratitude involves recognising and appreciating the positive aspects of life, expressing thankfulness, and cultivating a sense of abundance and contentment.

Empathy. Developing empathy entails the ability to understand and share the feelings and experiences of others. It involves actively listening, seeking to understand, and responding with compassion.

Authenticity. Embracing authenticity means being true to oneself and expressing genuine thoughts, feelings, and values. It involves living in alignment with one's true self rather than conforming to societal expectations or seeking approval.

Open-mindedness. Being open-minded involves being receptive to new ideas, perspectives, and experiences. It entails a willingness to challenge preconceived notions, engage in constructive dialogue, and embrace lifelong learning.

Collaboration. Valuing collaboration means fostering cooperation, teamwork, and mutual support. It involves recognising the collective strength and diverse contributions of individuals to achieve common goals.

These values can serve as a starting point for personal reflection and exploration. If you plan to take this to your team and develop team values, these are the most common:

Accountability, collaboration, honesty, transparency, innovation, learning, growth, feedback, open communication, mindfulness, ownership, collective learning and shared knowledge, relationships, and connections.

Mission and vision

In the landscape of our lives, vision and mission serve as the guiding threads, illuminating the path towards purposeful existence.

I experienced this profound truth through my transformative experience when I realised that I had lived the last nine years of my life in the amygdala (middle part of our brain) in fight-or-flight mode.

Upon the revelation that I need not conform, but rather could stand out, my entire world underwent a seismic shift.

Stepping out of the realm of primal survival instincts, I ventured into a heart-centred space of creation. Stepping beyond basic survival instincts, I moved into a space filled with heart and creativity. In this place, guided by intuition, my genuine vision and life's purpose showed themselves in their pure beauty.

With clear understanding, my vision statement came forth—simple and determined. It became a guiding light, a clear expression of my special purpose that felt unquestionably right. Soon after, my mission statement followed naturally, extending from my new-found clarity. In this realisation, there was no uncertainty or concern. Every word, every goal, felt genuine, resonating through the depths of my being. It wasn't just a statement; it was a promise to my inner self.

The significance of this revelation extends far beyond my personal narrative. It is the blueprint for profound transformation, the catalyst for stepping away from the confines of fear, doubt, and scarcity. As we guide our clients through this sacred process, we aim not for them to merely dream, but to see, feel, experience, and know, for within that knowing lies the profound shift from uncertainty to unwavering trust. It is a metamorphosis, a rebirth, as they witness the truth within themselves and deeply feel what is right and true. This authenticity becomes the foundation upon which they build their lives, careers, and relationships.

In this space of heart-centred creation, we witness the emergence of an unshakable foundation forged from the crucible of truth. Here, fear gives way to trust, doubt surrenders to clarity, and scarcity transforms into abundance. The most important part of this transformation is feeling an emotional experience of authenticity and vision.

The journey towards authentic vision and mission is not just a step towards success; it is a quantum leap towards a life of purpose and fulfilment. For when we know our destination, every step becomes purposeful, every action an expression of our truest selves. And in this knowing, we find not only success but a profound sense of wholeness and alignment with the universe.

From this inner space, guided by true vision and authenticity, we can start leading people.

How mission and vision influence our thinking

Mission and vision statements are powerful tools that shape our thinking patterns and mindset by providing a clear sense of purpose, direction, and motivation. We create a vision, but at the same time, we remove attachments.

Visions and goals are guides for learning opportunities and growth. It is not the final destination, because the vision will grow, change and transform with us.

Personal vision and purpose are important, and the best way to stay inspired is to align your vision with your values.

Mission and vision statements articulate the fundamental purpose and goals of an individual, organisation, or collective effort. They define the "why" behind our actions and decisions. By having a clear sense of purpose, our thinking becomes focused, and we can align our thoughts and actions with our desired outcomes.

Mission and vision statements establish specific goals and aspirations that we strive to achieve. They help us set targets and create a roadmap for success. This goal-orientation influences our thinking patterns by directing our attention towards actions and strategies that support the fulfilment of our mission and vision. We stay focused, but not only that, we actually stay inspired if the vision and mission are aligned with our true purpose.

Knowing our vision or goals often allows for long-term perspectives and broader horizons. By embracing a long-term mindset, our thinking becomes more strategic, forward-thinking, and proactive, enabling us to make decisions that align with our long-term goals.

Mission and vision statements are grounded in core values and principles. They provide a framework for decision-making, as we evaluate choices based on their alignment with our values. This values-based thinking promotes ethical considerations, integrity, and a sense of coherence in our actions.

By having a clear mission and vision, we develop a positive mindset that focuses on possibilities, resilience, and the belief that we can make a difference. They guide our thinking by identifying what truly matters and what we need to prioritise. This focus on what is essential helps us make informed decisions and avoid distractions or activities that do not align with our mission and vision.

Knowing our authentic vision and mission often requires continuous improvement, learning, and adaptation. They foster a growth mindset by encouraging us to embrace change, seek new opportunities, and learn from experiences. This mindset of growth and adaptability influences our thinking by promoting curiosity, resilience, and a willingness to step out of our comfort zones.

Now you have an idea of how we can set our thinking and your team's collective thinking up for success. I share more practical values, beliefs, and vision tools in later chapters of this book. I would suggest taking those practical exercises and creating a short workshop with your team or using it for yourself for your personal career and success.

E—Emotional level

Emotional fitness, encompassing awareness, self-awareness, social awareness, relationships with ourselves and others, self-effectiveness, and meaning, is vital for both individuals and groups or teams.

Awareness

Awareness is like having a radar for everything around us, both inside and outside. It's about tuning into the world, noticing the details, and understanding the bigger picture. It's like being fully present in the moment, taking in all the sights, sounds, and feelings without judgement or distraction.

In terms of emotional fitness, awareness is the starting point. It's about recognising not only our own emotions but also the emotions of others. It's like being attuned to the subtle shifts in the emotional climate of a room. This awareness gives us a deeper understanding of the dynamics at play and empowers us to respond thoughtfully.

Think of it as having a wide-angle lens on life. We see not just what's directly in front of us, but also the broader context. This broader perspective allows us to make more informed decisions, navigate complex situations, and connect more deeply with those around us.

In a nutshell, awareness is the foundational skill that underpins emotional fitness. It's like having a superpower that allows us to engage with the world in a more profound and meaningful way.

Self-awareness

Self-awareness is the foundation of emotional fitness. It involves understanding our emotions, strengths, weaknesses, values, beliefs, behaviours, and triggers. By developing self-awareness, we gain insight into our own reactions and behaviours, enabling us to better regulate our emotions and make conscious choices. Self-awareness helps us contribute authentically, understand our impact on others, and effectively manage our emotions within a team or group setting. Awareness is like turning on a light in the deepest corners of our inner world. It's about really seeing and understanding ourselves—our emotions, our reactions, and the underlying currents that shape our experiences. It's a bit like being a detective, but instead of solving a mystery, we're uncovering the layers of our own being.

This quality is the cornerstone of emotional fitness. Without it, it's like trying to navigate a dark room without any sense of direction. When we're aware, we can make sense of our emotions, even the tricky ones, and respond to life from a place of wisdom and clarity. It's the difference between being tossed around by the waves or skilfully steering our own ship.

Imagine being able to recognise when a certain situation triggers discomfort, and instead of reacting, we pause, take a breath, and choose our response. That's the power of awareness. It's a tool that transforms us from passengers to captains of our own emotional journey.

In essence, awareness isn't just an aspect of emotional fitness; it's the very foundation upon which it stands. It's the flashlight that guides us through the labyrinth of our emotions, allowing us to navigate with confidence, resilience, and a deep understanding of ourselves.

Social awareness

Social awareness refers to the ability to understand and empathise with the emotions, needs, and perspectives of others. It involves being attuned to social dynamics, non-verbal cues, frequencies, or energies, and understanding others' communication styles, core needs, or cultural contexts. Social awareness enables individuals to navigate relationships effectively, build trust, and demonstrate empathy and respect towards others. Within a team or group, social awareness fosters open communication, collaboration, and a sense of belonging. The foundation of social awareness is observation and understanding.

Relationships within and with others

Relationships within and with others involve using emotional intelligence to establish and nurture healthy and productive relationships. It encompasses effective communication, conflict resolution, active listening, mindfulness, and the ability to build rapport and trust. When individuals within a team or group possess strong relationship management skills, it fosters positive dynamics, cooperation, and a supportive environment where collective goals can be achieved. You can learn more about rapport, trust, mindfulness, and communication in later chapters.

Self-effectiveness

Self-effectiveness refers to the ability to regulate and control one's emotions and behaviours. It involves resilience, adaptability, and the capacity to handle stress and setbacks constructively.

Effective self-management allows individuals to respond to challenges with composure, respond instead of reacting, make rational decisions, and maintain a positive attitude. In a team or group setting, self-management contributes to a harmonious work environment, increased productivity, and effective teamwork. Most importantly, it enables us to understand that thoughts create our emotions and feelings, and whenever we find ourselves in fight-or-flight mode, we can take it back to our mind and reflect on what we were thinking at that moment.

Meaning

Having a clear sense of **meaning** or **purpose** is like having a North Star guiding our emotional journey. It gives our actions and experiences a deeper significance, like each step is part of a larger, meaningful dance. It's what infuses our emotions with a sense of direction and fulfilment.

In terms of emotional fitness, meaning acts as a stabilising force. It provides a solid ground to stand on, even in the midst of turbulent emotions. When we know why we're doing what we're doing, it brings a sense of calm and purpose to our reactions.

Imagine facing a challenging situation, and in the midst of it all, you remember why it matters to you. That's the power of meaning. It's like a lifeline that keeps us anchored and focused, even when emotions are running high.

Furthermore, having a clear sense of purpose allows us to make decisions aligned with our values and long-term goals. It helps us filter through the noise of fleeting emotions and choose actions that are in harmony with our deeper intentions.

Values-based principles and purpose

Establishing **values** as an emotional compass provides a clear framework for decision-making and behaviour. Values guide individuals and groups in making ethical choices, resolving conflicts, and fostering a shared sense of purpose and direction. They serve as a common ground for collaboration, ensuring that actions align with shared principles. Values-based principles help teams develop a cohesive culture, enhance trust, and work towards common goals with integrity.

By prioritising emotional fitness and embracing self-awareness, social awareness, relationship management, self-management, and values-based principles, both individuals and groups can enhance their overall wellbeing, communication, collaboration and therefore results and performance in general. These aspects create an environment of understanding, trust, and mutual respect, enabling teams to thrive, achieve shared objectives, and adapt to challenges more effectively. These principles, in our cognitive and emotional level of change, create psychological safety and a great culture.

In the practical part of this book, you will find more detailed information about emotional fitness, how our brains work, and how we create our reality. I will take you deeper into your cognitive and emotional level by discovering what your values, beliefs, and motivators are and bring awareness to your self-management and emotional fitness.

B—Behavioural level

In the CEB (cognitive-emotional-behavioural) method I developed, the third part focuses on the behavioural level or behavioural aspect/expressions of one's thinking patterns and emotional aptitude. Based on our thinking patterns, we create our feelings and emotions. Based on our emotional state, we make great or bad decisions in everyday life or in our work. To deepen your understanding, I can give you a short example.

I can recall a highly stressful situation when I found myself running late for work and I had to start my presentation for potential clients on time. It was one of those mornings where everything seemed to go awry. My alarm failed to go off, and as I realised the time slipping away, a surge of stress washed over me. I needed to get to work promptly, but it seemed like time was slipping through my fingers.

In this high-stress scenario, my emotions were in turmoil. I felt a mix of anxiety, frustration, and a strong sense of urgency. The pressure to arrive at work on time was immense, and my mind was racing as I brainstormed ways to expedite the process.

In this heightened state of stress, I made a hasty decision. I left my USB stick at home.

Without considering the consequences, I chose to take an unfamiliar shortcut to save precious minutes. However, little did I know that this shortcut was under construction, leading to unexpected road closures and traffic congestion. Instead of saving time, my decision only exacerbated the situation, leaving me feeling even more rushed and stressed.

Reflecting on this experience, I realised that my emotional state and the urgency I felt had a significant impact on my decision-making. In the midst of the chaos, I failed to think rationally and weigh the potential outcomes. The stress overwhelmed my ability to consider alternative options or take a moment to gather my thoughts.

This personal experience served as a valuable lesson, reminding me of the importance of managing stress and maintaining a clear mind in high-pressure situations. It highlighted the need to pause, take a deep breath, and assess the situation before making decisions. By prioritising self-care and cultivating a calm mindset, I have since learnt to approach stressful situations with greater composure and make more thoughtful choices.

I now can be in a very similar situation and will feel such stressful moments in a different way.

My experience is different because I am aware of the energy needed for my prefrontal cortex to keep me thinking straight.

I take a deep breath and think, *What can I do right now to change the situation? How can I make it better and avoid any problems, and how can I make our potential clients feel welcomed and taken care of?*

You can only change your response.

Now, I would call my assistant and ask her to prepare breakfast and coffee for the clients or take them through the office and introduce them to the team that will work with them. I would call the best communicator in our office to create a bit of friendly conversation as a warm-up. In the end, being late will actually have a positive impact on our meeting and their decision. Creating this type of environment, where people know how to deal with stress and emotional pressure, will only help encourage healthy behaviours and habits.

To fully address the behavioural level, it is important to consider various factors, including processes, habits, and what creates actions. Here are some elements to consider.

Processes

Processes refer to the systematic and organised methods or procedures that individuals or groups follow to accomplish tasks or achieve goals. Examining and optimising processes can contribute to more efficient and effective behaviours. This involves analysing workflows, identifying bottlenecks, and implementing improvements to enhance productivity and outcomes.

Then consider introducing values-aligned processes to create a great culture and behaviour. Also, processes have to be set up to help us demonstrate our values and principles in day-to-day operations or day-to-day life. Processes are changing behaviours; that's why they need to be based on alignment with the desired cognitive and emotional levels of the team and culture. Processes need to support our qualitative part of "being".

Habits

Habits are recurring patterns of behaviour that have become automatic through repetition. They significantly influence our daily actions and can be beneficial or detrimental. Habits can be expressed in processes. Assessing and cultivating positive habits can promote desired behaviours and support personal and professional growth. Breaking or modifying unhelpful habits is also important for behaviour change and improvement.

Actions

Actions are the tangible behaviours and choices we make in specific situations. It is essential to examine and evaluate our actions in light of our cognitive and emotional processes. We need to clarify qualitative C and E levels of actions to create great execution and positive results. This involves reflecting on the alignment between our intentions, values, and the actual behaviours we exhibit. Adjusting our actions to be more congruent with our goals and values can lead to positive change and growth.

Feedback

Feedback and measurement are important components of behavioural change. Regularly assessing and providing feedback on behaviours allows for course-correction and improvement. Utilising quantitative or qualitative measures can help track progress, identify areas for growth, and motivate individuals or teams to sustain desired behaviours. We will talk about agility tools and how you can utilise those tools to create great positive sustainable habits and measure them.

Rewards

Implementing reinforcement strategies and appropriate rewards will strengthen and sustain desired behaviours. Again, we are going back to processes. Recognising and celebrating achievements and progress can reinforce positive actions, fostering motivation and a sense of accomplishment.

By considering these elements—processes, habits, actions, environment, feedback and measurement, and reinforcement—individuals and groups can create a supportive framework for behavioural change, growth, and sustainable improvement. These components work together to enhance behaviours, promote positive habits, and optimise performance in alignment with the cognitive and emotional development of qualitative components of great culture and psychological safety.

What is conscious leadership 6.0 methodology all about?

Leadership 6.0 is a framework for personal development, growth, and leadership development. It is an important set of skills for influence, positive impact, and the integration of leadership success flow, a culture of kindness, and processes.

Leadership 6.0 is based on my personal experience, personal transformation, and testing and utilising the transformation of my clients in a high-stress environment. I utilise a lot of knowledge from my business career, my personal and spiritual journey, tools that worked for me and for my clients, and also some acquired wisdom and knowledge from my mentors from various areas such as neuro-linguistic programming, neuroscience, behavioural science, psychology, emotional intelligence, mental agility, and qualitative, values-aligned thinking.

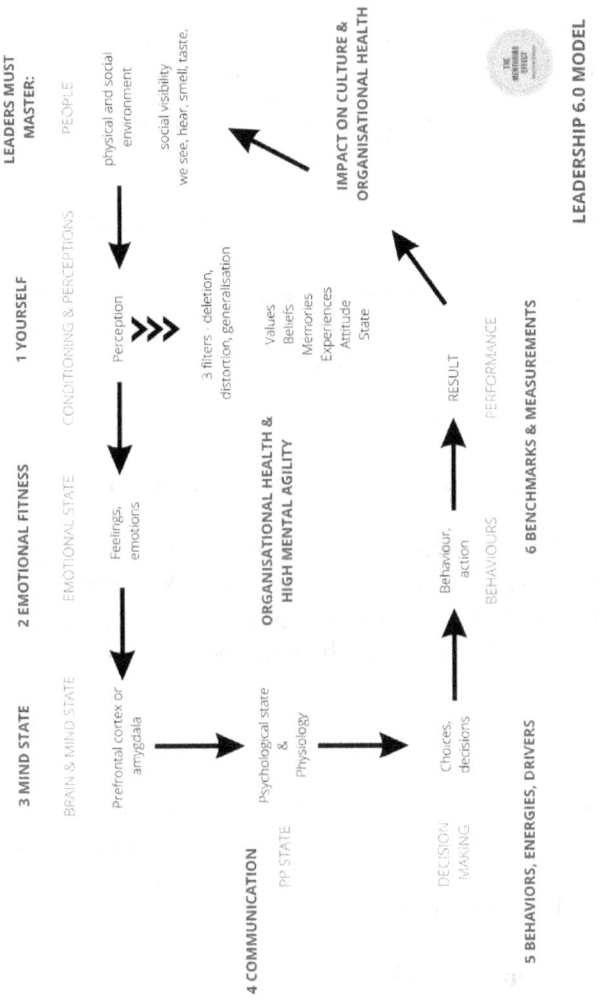

You're there to help your team to think in a way that:

- seeks to challenge their own beliefs and attitudes about what's possible
- allows them to own their role and take responsibility

- boosts their personal performance
- gives them more job satisfaction
- encourages them to contribute to the improvements and innovations in the organisation
- guides them in how to solve problems in a way that demonstrates good judgement and thought for consequences
- allows them to think of others and the impact decisions have on them
- allows them to lower their stress and improve their wellbeing.

Leadership is a vital management function that helps to direct an organisation's resources for improved efficiency and the achievement of goals. Effective leaders provide clarity of purpose and motivate and guide the organisation to realise its mission. Regardless of your position, understanding the role of leaders can help you contribute more meaningfully to the accomplishment of your company's objectives.

What is the importance of impact and leadership?

One of the most important functions of a leader is to provide a vision for the company. The leader explains the vision, takes people with them towards this one united vision, and helps people to co-create and understand what must be done to achieve it while helping them to learn and grow through the process.

While an organisation may have people with various talents and capabilities, it is leadership that harnesses individual efforts, strengths, and capabilities towards the collective goal. By understanding the team members and dynamics in the team, inspiring and motivating teams and coordinating personal actions for the advancement of a common goal, leaders help their companies achieve excellent results.

Why do we need leaders?

Teams often comprise multi-talented individuals who have the right skills and experience to deliver results, but most organisations still choose a team leader to direct the energy of the members for greater effectiveness. A leader is here to create an environment where people can thrive, innovate, and achieve. A leader is a facilitator of a great culture and organisational health.

Purpose

Leaders have a clearer understanding of the team's purpose and what it must do to make it a reality. Effective leadership not only guides but also identifies, understands, and communicates the organisation's vision to inspire others to support them to achieve objectives. During the designing and implementation of a project, it is the leader who ensures every team member understands their role and provides an enabling environment to help them perform at their best. Even better, leaders should know what each member's strengths are and help them to utilise their strengths in the best way for the project. Not only that, but leaders should also teach others how to do it and increase awareness about the energy and capabilities of the team members. All members should know about their strengths because they can help each other without the leader's ongoing daily involvement.

Promote values

Team leaders can encourage others to take up essential values vital for the organisation's success, but what is more sustainable is to create team values—create a great team culture that is based on team members' values. Values are their compass. Values drive behaviours every day. Standards such as accountability and values such as taking responsibility, transparency, and clarity when things go wrong can also make the organisation a better place for employees and clients.

Promote creativity

Team leaders can also foster an atmosphere of creativity in an organisation. While leaders help others see the vision of the business, they can also provide more flexibility for how employees do their work. This can help produce new insights on how to perform tasks, make decisions, and deliver on projects, improving efficiency and productivity.

The mindset of a great leader

- In leadership and life, mindset is the foundation of success. A growth mindset thrives on challenges and sees failure as a stepping stone to greater achievements. Leaders with a growth mindset embrace opportunities to learn and develop, viewing setbacks not as indicators of their limits but as catalysts for growth. For example, when faced

- with a project setback, they analyse what went wrong, learn from it, and adapt strategies for future success. They don't get stuck and emotional about the setback.
- Conversely, a fixed mindset is constrained by self-imposed limits. Leaders with this mindset may perceive failure as a reflection of their abilities, leading to avoidance of challenges or reluctance to take risks. For instance, they might resist delegating tasks, fearing that others won't meet their standards, thus limiting team growth and innovation.
- Great leaders are inspired by the success of others, viewing it as a source of motivation and learning. They celebrate others' achievements and seek to understand the strategies behind their success, integrating valuable insights into their own leadership approach. In contrast, jealousy of others' success reflects a fixed mindset, where people and leaders may feel threatened or undermined by others' accomplishments, hindering collaboration and personal growth.

Attributes of a great leader

Some attributes I really value and admire in some leaders that I like to model are:

- awareness of self, inner world, moods, and emotions, and their impact on day-to-day life
- ability to live day-to-day consciously and intentionally
- generosity
- discipline and consistency
- humanity
- vulnerability
- honesty and transparency
- a strong understanding of themselves, their teams, and the people around them
- confidence and self-trust
- being an example—living their values with no excuses and guiding others to live their values

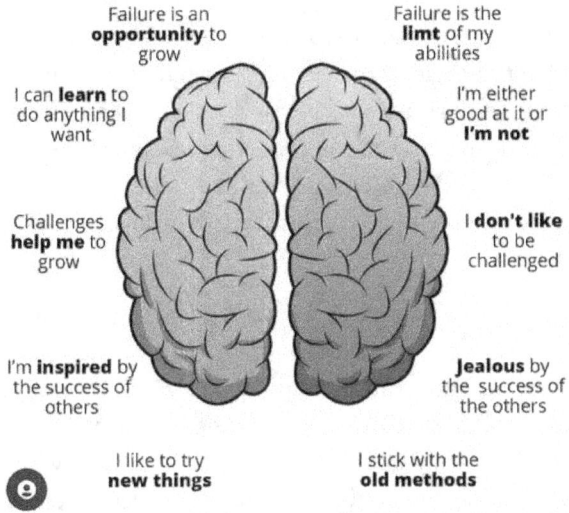

- exercising strategic thinking and sound decision-making—no rush or last-minute fixes
- practising integrity (walking your talk), intent (motives of mutual benefit), capabilities (abilities that inspire confidence), and results (your track record)
- having emotional intelligence, self-awareness, and a capacity to listen and assist
- caring deeply and helping without asking; serving
- encouraging a climate of truth, brutal facts, feedback, autopsy, and ways to learn
- leading with questions, knowing a lot about coaching questioning
- having the ability to inspire, develop, guide, and challenge others to help them grow

- creating an environment where people can grow, thrive, innovate, contribute, and learn.

Research conducted before the pandemic identified three important attributes leaders must possess in 2030. Coming out on top was the ability to be "innovative", followed by being "adaptive to change" and "collaborative across business".

When I was hired to lead two teams of twenty-five people, my biggest challenge was that there had been no trust built at that stage and no relationships or understanding, because I was there as a new leader and no-one knew me. I realised that there was no trust in leadership because they had been lied to and tricked by the leader before me. I felt like I stepped into a lion's cage and no-one knew where it would go. I went back to basics: relationships and trust-building. But how?

Well, it is the same as at school when you want to make new friends and understand who is around you—just start by being honest and open. I shared honestly with my team how the situation was uncomfortable not only for them but also for me. I suggested making it easier for all of us and starting with transparency and honesty. I had a few individual meetings with team members to introduce us to each other and ask them if they were open to having a short team meeting and open discussion about us working together as a team.

I shared my experience from the first few days and also shared that I met people in the organisation who I had had little disagreements with from the beginning. Well, I asked them for their opinion and asked them to tell me about the past year and their experience. After this conversation, where I was mostly a listener, I asked how they wanted to have their work and workplace for the next twelve months—what changes they would love to see, what they would like to keep, and what they wanted for themselves.

I shared that we could try it together or we could have a really bad time together and that it was up to us to make it easier. Everyone was on board, and everyone was happy to share their experiences and visions. We went for a great dinner afterwards and openly talked about our personal lives as well, which I truly didn't expect. That gave me a bit of hope that things could change and trust could be rebuilt.

I believe this was the best choice for my introduction. **Transparency and honesty** set us up for success and, after a few weeks of discussions, we felt like we were one and we could solve all the problems or issues that came our way.

Open conversation is a great start, but as leaders, we must have great **listening and facilitation skills** to facilitate a great discussion with positive results.

The pandemic has accelerated the need for leaders to develop essential skills called "soft skills" in the past. Skills like communication, listening, questioning, facilitating, speaking, problem-solving, decision-making, creativity, motivation, empathy, relationship management, negotiation, and so on. These are skills that leaders need in remote environments to lead employees through uncertainty while encouraging productivity to achieve good business outcomes. But there is even more to this. There is another level of being and living. There is consciousness and intentional action or behaviours. There is a part of leadership we never truly talked about: self-love, self-care, self-exploration, and understanding on a deeper level. There is a part of leadership where we need to understand that, as a leader, what you feel is what you project. You can easily be a bottleneck to your team's growth if you are projecting fears, stress, or anxiety even though you tried to pretend all is fine.

I know it is too much to process, but trust me. Operating from the space of your higher self will take you to the highest possible performance and mission.

But where to start?

We need to start with self-awareness, emotional intelligence, and understanding our emotions, moods, needs, behaviours, and triggers. For that, we created our Break that Pattern program to help you understand all of them and learn all of those skills by practising and implementing them into your daily life. But I will try to help as much as possible by writing a few pages about it. Based on the integration of all those shifted levels of awareness, moods, emotions, and behaviours, you will get feedback from your environment straight away. You will also be able to measure it.

This program requires your full attention and accountability with your action and integration. I don't think I have to mention that without your commitment, nothing would change.

Learning and empathy

A leader must constantly ask what they and the organisation are learning from the current crisis, as well as focus on future opportunities. I remember the statement that someone said: "A crisis is a terrible thing to waste." I love it.

Learning comes from listening. If people or leaders are attuned to themselves and others, to the unique challenges of their staff, customers and communities, they can make positive changes in areas such as team performance, customer experience, employee experience, work culture, strategy, and results.

Learning from circumstances and responding with ease is the most important skill to have and it separates you from unsuccessful people who delve into mistakes and beat themselves up for doing or saying something wrong or failing. Your positive attitude and response to those will make the biggest change in your progress.

Learning coupled with listening is empathy, which is highly important for the leaders of today or tomorrow.

Empathy goes beyond listening to hearing these stories. Seek to understand how your employees are feeling. Create a psychologically safe place to share, which may include one-on-one informal conversations, team huddles, social media forums, or town hall meetings. In these settings, show empathy by sharing personal stories and showing compassion for the feelings the crisis evokes in others. This doesn't mean you need to show sympathy; this means you need to listen to what truly is going on. Sometimes people will say something but they mean something different. By active and conscious listening, you will know what that hidden word is, what the hidden thoughts or emotions they don't show are, and even if they say something out loud, you will know it is not true.

By empathising and hearing the stories of frontline staff, leaders have power. Armed with the knowledge of what makes employees tick, what improves their working day, and what can facilitate the best outcomes, leaders can inform decisions both big and small, and an organisation can become an unstoppable force.

Exercise

ACTION EXERCISE:

1. Write down what leadership means to you. What was your unconscious bias?

2. Write down what you would like to be known for and what attributes you want to demonstrate as a great leader.

3. If you are working with a group or team—please organise a fifteen-minute meeting with your team members (maybe over lunch) and discuss together what the attributes of a great leader are and what they would like to see in their leader and team members. Ask them a simple question: "What is important to you?"

4. Reflect daily: "What went well? What can I do better?" and "Who was I today? How did I show up? Is there any space for improvement?"

Start with knowing and understanding yourself

You are a product of your past conditioning. How you got where you are is a function of biology, psychology, your past, experience, the culture you were raised in, the way you were perceived, the media you consumed, the way you spent your day, the books you read, the conversations you had, and what you focus on all day long, as well as endless other factors that are so important although we barely notice them.

In terms of where you are at right now, what you didn't experience is as significant as what you did experience and have come to accept as truth.

The most important factor is your predominant feeling or mood.

So, the question is, are you aware of the experiences, truths, ideas, beliefs, moods, emotions, perceptions, values, and choices that will empower you and help you to live your awesome life and become a great human being, a great friend, a great partner, or outstanding conscious leader?

If you want to find out all about yourself and live your authentic self with a sense of deeper purpose and alignment, you must take full responsibility for your own life, emotions, thoughts, decisions, and actions.

Now, we will start with the concept that your life and your environment are an expression of your perception and who you are.

You are a creator of your circumstances. You are a powerful human being even without knowing. Every second, every minute of the day, your predominant moods, emotions, and thoughts create your future for the next years ahead.

You're not experiencing life as it is, you are experiencing life as *you are*. Everything you see around you is based on the lens that you use to see the world. Those lenses are filters, such as beliefs, values, memories, emotions, experiences, and all your past conditioning based on what you saw and felt during your life.

Basically, it all started with a "premise" creation. This is almost like the original program, the first program in your brain based on your first seven years of life experiences. Most of our programs and conditioning are created at that time, sometimes during the time we can't consciously remember. But what I realised is that your body, your spiritual and emotional body, remembers every event and experience. I can help my clients to recall the feeling of the experience, even if it's the first month of their life or even when they were born. This experience you are not even aware of can create your entire life, results, or circumstances the way you don't want. But somehow, it's happening.

Now, at the age of thirty or fifty, we are basically living on autopilot based on this program that was created by the age of seven, without realising we evolved emotionally and spiritually.

So many of my clients, when they start working with me, are in their forties or fifties realising they lost their mojo, lost their passion, and ask, "How come I feel this way? How did I arrive at this? I have enough money and a great position or business, but I thought I would feel different and I would be in a different place. Why am I not feeling joy or feeling a bit unsettled all the time?" or "Why am I feeling impatient and like I am in a hurry all the time?"

Well, this is where the work starts. You need to break the pattern of your old self living life on autopilot, on the conditioning and program you developed in your childhood or in your teens. Instead, you need to let your mind, emotions, and spirit know you actually evolved and you don't need the old patterns because they don't serve you.

Your life is a reflection of past experiences, memories, values, beliefs, attitudes, moods, emotions, feelings, choices, actions, and expectations. To feel empowered, you need to be aware of these truths first:

1. You are responsible for your life, your choices, your responses, your thoughts, feelings, and emotions.
2. You are a creator.

3. You have feelings and emotions inside you and some of them are hidden, so you need to bring awareness to those because they are influencers of your future.
4. You don't lie to yourself. You give yourself an honest awareness about your strengths and dark side or where you need to lift your game.
5. You don't beat yourself up for your weaknesses; you accept and work daily on improvements.
6. You are the catalyst for the change you want to see in your life, leadership, or team (stop wishing, wanting, and hoping).
7. You are living fully and, on this journey, you will figure it all out; give yourself time.
8. Your circumstances are a direct reflection of your thoughts, attitudes, and emotions.
9. Your subconscious doesn't think but feels. Feelings and emotions are your compass, and by being aware of those, you know where you are heading.
10. You make mistakes; you learn, you improve, and then you move on—don't wait till you have it right; don't regret and don't go back.
11. No-one has to change for you to live your life. Everyone is the way they should be.
12. Everyone deserves love. All we can do is become a better version of ourselves and teach, guide, mentor, coach, and challenge others to become a better version of themselves.

Success Principles

Now we will talk about success principles that have been studied by authors and psychologists for years. I learnt this from my mentors Tony Robbins, Jim Rohn, Stephen Covey, and so many more. I put together my own success principles that guided my transformation and led me to personal fulfilment, purpose, and greater results.

Those success principles are the best combination of principles that helped me and my clients to grow and evolve awareness and sustainable change.

Master your emotions and mood

The most important foundation for mastering your life and creating change is to master your predominant emotions or feelings. Your internal state or mood will dictate your future results. I can give you a great example of my client's internal world and the changes he experienced. He came to one of our sessions unsettled and I felt the emotion in the air. I looked at him and asked calmly, "Hmm—I can see something is going on right now with you. How are you feeling?"

He looked at me with an acknowledgement that I could see it. "Alex, I feel a bit unsettled, a little anxious, disheartened, bothered. I had a conversation with one of the CEOs of a potential client and he decided to join us. He knew this was the best solution for them. But yesterday, he said they are too busy to finalise the project and the right time will probably be next year. It has happened with two potential clients in the past two days, and I feel a bit anxious. I also was considering how I could grow this project and, with maximum effort, it will still give me only 50% of the income I wanted to create."

I asked him to reflect on what was going on inside him and how and what he was making this mean. He made the one little "no" mean more than it was. He allowed this little "no" to dictate and define his future.

We continued with the interventions, and he made himself a different person when he left the session. He realised how he was creating this reality for himself. From that day on, he had a little task to do, and it was using our breath exercise and recalibration model before the day started or anytime during the day he needed to reset his mood. He is now creating his own better and more positive circumstances. The following weeks became the best weeks of his life. He shifted his mood and emotions. Let's get into the details of this.

If you allow any small failure, mistake, or little rejection to define you and irritate you, you create a state of anxiety and self-doubt or doubt about life working for you, and that is pointing out that you are not in a state of being in the right state or being big enough for your business. There are always negative events in your life, but what matters the most is your response to them. You decide what you make it mean. Is it a learning curve or is it a problem that identifies you? If it becomes a strong negative feeling or emotion, it may stop you from achieving what you want. It will create an emotional state from which it is hard to work and achieve. Why does this matter?

People—potential clients, employees, or friends—all feel you. When your predominant feeling is fear, you act on it. Your facial expression changes and your body language and your tonality or language sound different, so people feel you are scared or you become a chaser who wants something from them.

The moment you change your emotions to gratitude, love, and compassion, and you realise you are good enough, life is perfect and has perfect timing, and you see that you are here to serve a higher purpose, your emotions change. How people perceive you changes, how people respond to you and how you respond to them changes, and each meeting becomes a deeper, valuable moment of your life.

Know your outcome—begin with the end in mind

Why is that important? I can give you an example from sales training with my client. We aim to do forty sales calls a day—stage one of our strategy. We couldn't get through ten. I realised there was no clear outcome and process to the call strategy—there was no clear understanding of what the outcome and expectation from this first so-called cold call were. There was a high expectation of sales from the calls, when we all know that is not how cold calls work. We started to have more success when we clarified the focus, intention, and outcome of the call, and that was to get a twenty-minute meeting with the person on the call just to get to know the person on the other side, not to close the deal straight away. If you turn your first call, or any conversation, into a sales call, you have already lost.

Another great metaphor for this is a taxi driver: when you don't know the address, you will never arrive at the destination. If you only know the name of the city, you will find yourself cruising around and will never stop. You need the street name and the number to arrive where you want to arrive.

How many people here have set goals in their leadership development and, after a while, they failed or they lost focus? A goal without purpose and real emotional connection means nothing. It's just a number without importance. How many people here have the exact number/financial results they want to create in business or their career? And do you have the place where you want to create it? Start focusing on details—they are important to you. Don't just make it up because you have to. Make it mean something to you. Visualise.

And do you have steps to create it? You have to know your outcome, results, your goal—where you are aiming.

How will you be able to become a great leader if you are not sure what the end product of yourself looks like?

Do you have your goal or outcome set up from authentic space or is it just something that sounds "cool"?

Zig Ziglar said, "If you aim for nothing, you will hit it thousands of times."

We usually have a lot of language about what our problem is, what's wrong, and what we don't want. But how can we speak the language that we want in life? So many people just go through life and live what is shown. If it's a bad day, it's a bad day, and sometimes, they have a good day—that just happens. They take no responsibility for what is happening. Remember, you are a creator. If there is fear of setting the goal that you see for yourself, go back to success principle number one and reset your emotional state. Don't change your goal because you are scared—change your fear and attitude.

ACTION EXERCISE:

1. Intentionally think about and write down the answer to "What am I actually aiming to achieve?"
2. What would make this an outstanding day, week, month, or year?
3. Who do I need to become? What do I need to feel daily? What do I need to do today to become one step closer to my ideal self?
4. Instead of focusing on problems, we switch and focus on what we are aiming for. Shift focus to your ideal outcome.

Embrace bold action—be proactive and prioritise

When you know where you are aiming—what your big goal is, who you need to become—what is your first "massive" action? What is the step to take to improve? Start with yourself.

Don't judge; don't put any energy into those negative thoughts. Be aware of them and let them go. In this grand expedition of life, knowing your destination is the compass. What's your North Star, your grand ambition? Once you've painted this vivid picture, the next step is crystal clear. It's about taking that monumental first step towards improvement, beginning with the most important person—you.

Take a moment to dive into the technique of awareness, unravelling the enigma of your true self. Here, we acknowledge both our shadows and our brilliance. Every emotion, even the ones we're not fond of, finds its place without judgement. It's not about condemning them but recognising and releasing them. Find a way to take action. Look inwards to see what is holding you back and work through it. There is no-one else who has power over you, only you. Procrastination? Really? I'm sure you are beyond that and you don't allow this to bother you and be present in your life. Perfectionism is the way to procrastination. Nothing is perfect. Take imperfect action, because even if today you think something is perfect, that is not true tomorrow, anyway. Imperfect action is more important than staying stuck. Move, even with little steps; even one phone call today can change your tomorrow.

Operate from a physiology and psychology of excellence

Now, we know our emotions influence how we act and what decisions we make. Our physical state, on the other hand, is responding to and creating our attitudes, emotions, and thinking.

If you feel stuck or not in the mood, the fastest way to change it is to change your physiology. Take care of your health, meditate, and practise breathing exercises.

The best breathing exercise to calm your nerves is box breathing. I will mention more about this later on.

Here's a sacred truth: our physical state is the forge that shapes our mindset and attitude. Our wealth, our health, and our mental wellbeing all intertwine. There are moments when showing up for others, even if our spirits falter, is our sacred duty. It begins with physiology—a stance of power, an energised stride.

The next time inertia lingers and the thought of exercise feels daunting, take action. Put on that invigorating melody, straighten your posture, and step forth with confidence. Slip into those gym clothes and embark on your journey. Trust that, on this path, everything will shift and transform.

We need to take care of our wealth, health, and mental state. We are not always happy, and we are not always energised, but we need to turn up for our clients, family, team members, or friends sometimes even if we don't feel like it.

What works is physiology first. If you don't feel it mentally, decide to create physiology first and the mental excitement will follow that.

ACTION EXERCISE:

1. What does success mean to you?
2. What would make you succeed?
3. What makes someone stand out in a team environment or in a group?
4. What makes a leader truly an influencer?
5. Who do you want to model? How can you take those qualities and integrate them?

Chapter 3

CEB-3 Dimensions with 'Thinking Better'
STRATEGIC THINKING

During my studies and coaching, I integrated a few different lenses for thinking. I like the idea of having a lens or framework to think through. Basically, you can take every situation, area of your life, or result you want to achieve through various frameworks and questions.

I enjoyed thinking through the models. The majority of people think about what they need and ask questions like "What do I need to do to change the result or achieve something?" I found that was very limited thinking, so I implemented the "be-do-have" model. It goes like this: I ask first, "Who do I need to become? What do I need to do to achieve my goal?"

I also like to think through the critical alignment model, developed by Remi Pearson, which is a thinking model that is applicable to every situation in your life and work. It is a frame of thinking. **It is a critical thinking model. It helps with decision-making, problem-solving, recruitment strategies, how to approach leadership, how to approach managing others, how to give feedback, how to project manage, and how to measure performance. It is a fundamental model.** Ask yourself, can you articulate clear and tangible strategies about how you go about developing someone, how you create and execute your goals, how you achieve something, and how you solve the issue? What do you document, why do you do it the way you do, and how do you measure progress?

The majority of people in the world think through implementation. They are just doing and doing, acting automatically without thinking and without understanding their why. Acting subconsciously based on experiences and habits created in the past. Driving the same way to drop kids off at school, having coffee at the same coffee shop each morning, or creating task lists each day and just trying to finish the list without choosing priorities and asking themselves, "Why am I doing this? Is this really important and moving me closer to my vision? Is this truly moving a needle in my life or business?"

We are not questioning our actions anymore.

The way we dress, walk, talk, or act. I can give you one small trick my very successful client uses. He goes for an evening swim every day and he reflects and asks questions daily.

"What went well today and could be better?"

"What did I say or do that I can say or do better tomorrow?"

"Did I enjoy today, or can I do something differently so I feel joy and fulfilment every day?"

"Did I live my purpose today?"

"Did I add value to someone's life today?"

I like the critical alignment model because it helps you to ask your "why" and purpose first before you act. This model will help you to create quality around your actions, behaviours, and structures, understanding what your organisational priorities are. It will help you to co-create an amazing high-performance culture with your team. It will help you to create a strong foundation for a successful business and improve and achieve the desired results.

The critical alignment model is a model we are going to use for our leadership and culture development, and this model will oversee all conversations and our work and actions.

This model will help you to create and run effective meetings and achieve high performance.

Each dimension of this model has its own criteria. Let's quickly look at this so you can use it straight away.

Critical thinking

Making decisions can happen very easily and quickly with not-really-great results if we approach it from an implementation level without thinking or asking the right questions. What does that look like? Most people ask the wrong questions. They get ideas or they want to do or achieve something and they ask "*How* am I going to do it?" This is the first question from my clients.

What does this do? This question takes you to the logical analytical part of your brain and leaves creativity and intuition or purpose out of the question. So, you have limited capacity to solve "*how*".

If you start with *why* or *what*, you will move through solutions focused, with clarity, alignment, and better options. Be creative and you get more clarity.

Ask *why* we do what we do. *Why* do I want to achieve it? *What* exactly are we doing here? *What* do we want to be known for? *What* good in the world will this do? *What* attitude do we want to obtain? *What* would happen when we achieve it?

Stepping back to where we want to get in twelve months, *what* are the overarching types of thinking (environment) we need to bring into this and *what* strategies (structure) do we need to bring into it? After that, the team can develop *who* is doing what and *what* we need for the team. In summary: **the first level is how we think, the second level is what we should be thinking about and attending to, and integration, or the third level, is what we actually attend to and the people who attend to it.**

Quality of behaviours and thinking

The first level of thinking is the qualitative part of every decision, conversation, project, life, business, or team performance.

This part of the thinking patterns is the first and most important part to think of, the first question to ask ourselves and others is "Why? For what purpose?" and to understand what outcome we want.

We need to look at vision. Do we have a clear vision? Are our people fighting for the vision and mission or for their own desires?

Are we living by the rules of business? Do we understand passion is not enough and we need to combine this with skills and experience? Do we have a clear understanding of values and how we can demonstrate them every day? How can we breathe and live values? Standards? Attitudes? How do we bring our values to day to day life?

What are our beliefs? What do we believe about our brand, organisation, and leaders? Do we have a mission, and are we all inspired by the mission? Those elements become our blueprint.

How to bring quality of behaviours to systems

The second level or step in critical thinking is the mechanics of bringing systems and structure to these qualitative questions: what categories or criteria we need, the dimension of marketing sales delivery payments follow-up, and tech support. It could be within each division of the business. Each dimension can have its own operation manual and rules. Each can be broken down into mini-categories. For example, online marketing and offline marketing. Online marketing—social media marketing and Google® marketing. Google SEO and AdWords®. Google SEO website ranking, website updates and maintenance, and so forth. Each dimension breaks down into categories and each must be populated with rules, templates, checklists, and ops manuals. The more of those you have, the less freedom you give people to operate in implementation. It creates a level of accountability for all team players. Look at your hiring process and how to choose the right people, how you choose the best team players. It comes back to making a choice based on attitudes, behaviours and not only skills. That is the best option, but only if it's all values-aligned and outcome-aligned decisions.

How to integrate high-quality behaviour into your day-to-day

When we create some clear criteria for decision-making or thinking as an individual or team, we are able to make a process that serves these criteria. Now, to make it function, we need to integrate it and test what decisions we make as a result of our expectations, attitudes, and processes, what we do, and how we do it daily. I can give an example from the life of my client.

Jason was forty years old and a very successful man just taking over the CEO position of a multimillion-dollar company. He had a beautiful wife and kids and loved them deeply. He did everything for them, and others, to keep them happy. He came to me and said he was not sure, but he knew something was missing. He felt "weird". Those were his words. He felt down and flat, with no enthusiasm and sometimes just felt like he had no energy and no vitality, almost like being apathetic or numb. We started working together and we talked about his life experiences at a young age—in his teens and later in his career and relationships. There was so much adventure when he was young and also much trouble, disruption, and an abusive father who didn't really have too many nice words for him.

He had and still has an amazing mum and siblings, and they have a pretty good relationship. This all can look fine and normal, but putting together all the small experiences and moving forward twenty years later, seeing what he created seemed to be a little bit boring for him.

He was trying to find satisfaction, adventure, and variety in his work, but when he came to me, even his career was too settled for him. He felt down because he was bored. There was nothing to fight for, nothing to strive for, and there was a lot of uncertainty and he lacked a good relationship with success and money.

He was taught that successful people are bad people; you usually can't trust them and you better avoid them. Well, this little thought created a premise and limiting beliefs program that drove his life. He was able to grow even more and create bigger success with more variety and less boredom, but this little thought was stopping him from breaking free of that limit and going beyond his boundaries. He couldn't see it at the beginning, but the more we dug deeper into this realm, the more we realised that he was scared of success and he didn't want to be seen as a bad person.

He truly cared about what others thought about him too much instead of living his life fully. The issue there was that he seemed to be successful and had a pretty high position with all he wanted, but the truth was he felt down and unmotivated because he was so far away from living his full potential because of those subconscious limits he didn't know about.

I want you to think about this for yourself. If you feel like there is more to life, there is. If you feel like you are here for more and you should be somewhere much further along, that will be because you know that and feel it somewhere in your bones. That feeling is correct. If you feel like you are not living your purpose, you probably are not. If you feel like you can do more and you are more than capable of doing more but somehow you feel stuck, you definitely should do more and unlock those limits. Reprogram yourself. Don't settle for less if you know there is more for you and others. You were born with a purpose, and if you let your subconscious mind block your limits, you will never feel fulfilled.

We work through limiting beliefs about success, money, career, boredom, and work-life balance and see those concepts from different perspectives. Jason is now getting offers from other big companies to take over the CEO position and he is choosing his life and purpose instead of looking at money only. He asked the old owner to give him freedom and opportunities to do business with this company the way he wanted to. He stayed with that company, but he gained a massive level of freedom in decision-making. The future direction of the company is all in his hands, and he loves it. His financial situation improved so much that he bought a one-million-dollar house in ten minutes, and that was within only seven days of beginning our sessions.

You all have magic in your hands, and you have all the freedom in the world, you just need to decide to take it, act on it, and enjoy it.

If you change the quality of your thinking, everything will follow—change, transformation, and also results will follow.

The same rule applies to your team. If you help your people to think differently, you will transform the team's performance.

We focus on teamwork on three levels—always opening up with mindset and brain science and moving to emotional fitness and behaviour. When we finalise those conversations and let team members run their own progress and culture, they become a very different team from the perspective of dynamics, performance, and effectiveness.

All aspects of human beings—our thinking, emotions, behaviours, and energy—influence each other and influence other people. There is always a connection between people you can't cut off. There is ongoing interaction—invisible energetic and emotional interaction—that needs to be shifted in the work environment to achieve wellbeing, high performance, high effectiveness, and psychological safety. There is no other way to do it. If you take care of your people on all these levels and they understand the dynamics, they will automatically take care of the culture and improve communication and results.

Quality of relationships and connections are more important than quantity.

Chapter 4

Culture You Create
QUALITATIVE DIMENSION OF RESULTS

Culture is not just something that exists within the walls of a business—it permeates every part of our lives. Whether we realise it or not, we are constantly creating culture—at work, at home, in our relationships, and in the communities we engage with. Culture is the sum of our actions, intentions, and unspoken rules. It's the environment we shape and the emotional tone we set through our choices.

Culture reflects who we are and how we choose to show up in the world.

When we speak about building a business or leading a team, we often focus on strategies, systems, and structures. But what truly drives sustainable growth isn't just the operational aspects—it's the **emotional and energetic fabric** woven into the environment. The same principle applies to our personal lives. The way we engage with our families, how we treat our partners, and the example we set for our children all contribute to the culture we cultivate within our homes.

The truth is, **you cannot separate yourself from the culture you create.** Your leadership extends beyond business; it touches every aspect of your life. This is why **consciousness in leadership is essential.**

The power of culture in driving results

Culture is often described as "what happens when no one is watching". It's the energy that lingers after a meeting ends, the tone of the conversations that fill a room, and the emotional climate of a household after a disagreement.

Culture shapes:

- **How people feel** within the environment
- **How decisions are made** and whether they are fear-based or visionary
- **The level of trust, safety, and innovation** present in relationships and businesses
- **The energy of growth or stagnation** in any environment.

In business, culture can be the defining factor between **a thriving, engaged workforce** and one that feels disconnected and unmotivated. In personal relationships, culture can be the difference between **deep intimacy** and surface-level interaction. In communities, culture fosters either **collaboration and unity** or division and isolation.

Conscious leaders understand that culture is not a byproduct—it's a deliberate creation.

When we take ownership of the environments we shape, we unlock the ability to **lead from a higher state of awareness.**

How culture reflects your inner world

If the culture around you feels stagnant, uninspiring, or full of friction, the first place to look is **within yourself.**

Culture is often a reflection of the **internal state of its leader.**

- A leader who operates from scarcity and control creates environments of micromanagement and fear.
- A leader who embodies abundance and trust fosters creativity, autonomy, and innovation.

Likewise, in personal life, relationships mirror our internal landscape.

- If we carry unresolved emotional patterns, our relationships reflect disconnection.
- If we cultivate self-awareness and emotional openness, our personal connections deepen.

Your results are a reflection of the culture you've built around you.

If you find yourself achieving the same outcomes in business, health, relationships, or finances, it's an indicator that **the culture is reinforcing those patterns.** Culture, when left unchecked, becomes the silent architect of our limitations.

Creating conscious environments for limitless growth

Limitless growth cannot happen in environments ruled by outdated beliefs, toxic dynamics, or unconscious leadership. **To cultivate limitless results, you must consciously design environments that align with expansion, collaboration, and authenticity.**

This begins by reflecting on the key elements that shape the culture around you:

- **Vision**—What kind of environment do you want to create?
- **Purpose**—Why is this culture important to you and those around you?
- **Values**—What core values guide the interactions and decisions within this space?
- **Behaviours**—Are your daily habits reinforcing the culture you wish to build?
- **Communication**—Do people feel heard, valued, and safe to express themselves?

Example:

Consider a business owner whose vision is to foster innovation and creativity within their team. However, if the environment punishes mistakes, innovation is stifled. The stated values and the actual behaviours are in conflict, creating a **misaligned culture.**

The same applies at home. A parent may value openness and trust but respond to their child's mistakes with criticism, unintentionally cultivating fear rather than confidence.

Alignment between stated values and demonstrated behaviour is key to creating a conscious culture.

Unconscious aspects of culture

One of the most overlooked aspects of culture is **the hidden rules that shape behaviour.** These rules are rarely spoken but govern how people behave in environments—whether in the workplace or at home.

For example:

- A workplace that claims to value teamwork but rewards individual achievements creates a culture of competition.
- A family that expresses love but avoids difficult conversations develops a culture of emotional suppression.

Hidden rules reveal the unconscious aspects of culture. By uncovering and addressing them, we realign the environment with the limitless potential we seek to create.

Shifting culture through leadership

Culture is dynamic. It evolves every time we make a conscious decision to shift how we engage, lead, or respond. **Leaders are the architects of culture, and the culture they create influences everything.**

To shift culture:

1. **Model the behaviour you want to see**—Demonstrate the values you want to instil in others.
2. **Foster open communication**—Invite feedback, listen actively, and ensure all voices are heard.
3. **Acknowledge and address misalignment**—When actions contradict values, course-correct openly.
4. **Celebrate growth, not just results**—Recognise effort, creativity, and learning, not just performance.

Example:

A business owner noticed that team members feared voicing new ideas. By creating regular brainstorming sessions with no consequences for failure, the culture began to shift towards innovation and risk-taking.

In personal life, simply creating space for honest dialogue without judgment can transform the emotional climate of a relationship or family.

Expanding beyond business—culture as a way of life

Culture is not confined to businesses; it exists in every interaction, from the way you engage with strangers to how you handle setbacks.

- **In communities,** culture is reflected in how resources are shared and how people uplift or isolate one another.
- **In families,** culture determines how love is expressed, how conflict is navigated, and how each member feels valued.

By consciously cultivating **positive, growth-oriented environments** in all areas of life, you create ripple effects that extend beyond personal success—impacting those around you and shaping the broader collective.

To become limitless, create cultures that reflect the highest version of who you are becoming.

Final thought—you are the culture

Remember, culture is not separate from you—it's a reflection of your inner world. The environments you shape will always mirror your level of consciousness.

By embracing this truth, you step into the role of a **limitless creator,** capable of transforming not only your business but every aspect of your life.

The culture you create defines the legacy you leave. Make it one that elevates, inspires, and expands beyond boundaries. But how do you know your vision when you are not sure where you want to go yet and you feel a lack of purpose and direction?

Vision development

Okay, I will give you a short exercise first so that, if you are feeling lost, your team doesn't feel lost. Take the following exercise to your work team and start the conversation if needed. In the next section, I will talk about a personal vision.

EXERCISE: ACTION ITEM—CREATING A VISION OF CULTURE AND CHANGE:

Creating a conscious and intentional culture is one of the most powerful things you can do as a leader or business owner or within your family. Culture reflects the values you live by, the emotional tone you set, and the energy that flows through your environment. Whether you're leading a company, guiding a team, or shaping the dynamics at home, **a clear vision creates alignment, direction, and unity.**

An extraordinary vision of change doesn't have to be lengthy or complicated. It can be as simple as a concise, emotionally compelling statement that resonates deeply with those involved. Whether for your business or personal life, the goal is to inspire action, encourage reflection, and unify everyone toward a shared purpose.

Here's how you can craft your own vision of culture, one that can guide you and the people around you with clarity and intention:

1. Draft the first version of your vision

Humans are motivated by **emotions, stories, and meaningful goals.** When crafting your vision, consider including:

- **Numbers**—Quantifiable results or goals that provide structure.
- **Stories**—Personal anecdotes or real-life experiences that capture the essence of the vision.
- **Emotions**—Use emotionally driven language that reflects the heart of the vision (for example, words like *unity, trust, empowerment, or joy*).

The goal is to **make it simple yet powerful.** Speak from the heart, allowing the vision to evoke a sense of **purpose, connection, and hope.**

Example (business):

"We are creating an environment where creativity flows, mistakes are celebrated as learning opportunities, and every team member feels deeply valued and empowered to lead in their own way."

Example (family):

"Our family is a space of love, honesty, and open communication, where everyone feels safe to express themselves and support one another's growth."

2. Reflect with seven key questions

To ensure your vision aligns with your true values, start with the basics. Answer the following seven questions to elicit authentic insights:

1. What do we do as a team, business, or family?
2. What are we delivering to others (service, product, emotional support, collaboration)?
3. Why is this important to us?
4. How does our work or presence improve the lives of others?
5. How do our values show up in what we do daily?
6. What emotions do we want people to experience when they engage with us?
7. How will we hold ourselves accountable to this vision?

Once you've answered these questions, reflect deeper by asking:

- *Why is that important to our team, customers, or family members?*
- *And why does that matter to others and to the broader vision of who we want to become?*

Go deeper by repeating the "why" question multiple times. This technique helps **strip away surface-level answers** and reveals the core truth behind your actions and aspirations.

3. From reflection to refinement—creating a shared vision

Once you've dug deep and explored the layers of why your vision matters, it's time to involve the people around you—whether that's your team at work, your family, or a community group.

Ask:

- *How does this vision improve our collective lives?*
- *How does it help our clients, community, or each other thrive?*
- *What elements do we need to focus on together to make this a reality?*

The goal is to craft a shared vision that everyone feels ownership of. Culture is not built by one person—it emerges from consistent, **aligned action across the group.**

4. Finalising the vision—keep it short and powerful

Now that you have clarity, **distil your vision into one or two simple statements** that capture its essence.

- Keep it concise—ideally **no longer than half a page** or something that can be read and remembered within **sixty seconds.**
- Ensure it's **emotionally appealing and relatable.**
- **Reflect authenticity**—your vision must be grounded in truth, reflecting who you are and who you are becoming.

Example (team vision):

"We believe that innovation thrives in a culture of respect, collaboration, and curiosity. Our mission is to uplift one another, create without fear, and grow as leaders who inspire change."

Example (family vision):

"In our home, love, kindness, and honesty guide every interaction. We are committed to creating an environment where each person feels valued, supported, and deeply connected."

5. Why vision matters—tying it to conscious culture

The vision statement you create is more than just words—it becomes the **foundation of the culture you build.** It serves as a guidepost for decisions, a tool for resolving conflicts, and a reminder of the bigger picture.

- **In business,** a strong vision aligns teams, increases morale, and strengthens loyalty.

- **In families,** it nurtures emotional safety and reinforces shared values.
- **In communities,** it fosters unity and provides a sense of belonging.

When vision is lacking, culture drifts. People operate without clear direction, leading to misalignment, frustration, and disconnection. However, when a vision is present and alive in daily actions, **culture thrives.**

Living the vision—turning words into reality

A vision statement is not something you craft once and forget. It must be revisited, refined, and brought to life consistently.

To make it actionable:

- **Display it** somewhere visible—at home, in the office, or in shared spaces.
- **Integrate it** into meetings, family discussions, or daily rituals.
- **Celebrate moments** when the vision is embodied through actions.
- **Use it to realign** during challenging times, asking, *"Is this decision aligned with our vision?"*

Remember:

You are the architect of the culture around you. Whether in your business, home, or broader community, **your conscious effort to define and embody your vision creates ripple effects that inspire growth, trust, and connection.**

Culture isn't something we inherit—it's something we intentionally build, one action at a time.

Now, take a moment to reflect and begin shaping the vision that will guide you forward.

Journey within—your personal vision

Let's dive into how to become a greater leader or deepen understanding of who you are, why you do what you do, and what you want. This is a journey within. Building your vision doesn't work from a space of apathy, exhaustion, or being stuck. The first step in figuring out what you truly want, what you are made from, where you are coming from, where you're heading, and why you are here needs to come from a space of ease and inner peace.

It is actually possible to take yourself to this state at any time of the day. I will do my best to explain it all in detail, but if you still feel like it doesn't work well, please let me know. We can talk about it and I can guide you through to the state where you can feel connected to your purpose.

As I said, figuring out your true authentic vision, purpose, or what makes you tick will help you to guide yourself through the right career, health, or relationship path and, at the same time, will create a sense of fulfilment. To know who you are and what you want is the foundation of your life journey to success.

Success means different things for everyone. If I ask you what success really means to you, what would be your answer?

I saw so many definitions of success in my life, and the best guidance or definition I found was:

SUCCESS = ACHIEVEMENT + FULFILMENT

I believe I heard this from Russell Brunson, but I'm not sure who the original author of the idea is.

Let's go deeper into this. Success equals achievement. Well, we all want something, and we all do something that makes us feel good. We also have our values and little personal goals subconsciously written in our minds and bodies. It can be having a family or husband or wife, a job or business, or having a great healthy body or lifestyle. We all strive for something consciously or subconsciously. When you achieve it, you feel a sense of achievement and satisfaction. You feel that little dopamine hit, that excitement or butterflies in your stomach. But the next day, you already don't even know that you achieved something. That's why we need to add feelings into this and a deeper layer.

Fulfilment is the other half of this. Fulfilment is a different story. Fulfilment is how you feel about yourself when you are by yourself. There was a very huge shift in my world when I learnt this. Think about how perfect it is. You achieve something, you go home and you feel satisfied, but at the same time, you are happy with yourself, you acknowledge yourself, and you feel inspired to go to the next goal or thing that can improve your life or results even more. Because you feel that way, you can achieve anything in the world; you are satisfied with yourself and also you feel deep trust and respect towards yourself. Now, you feel great, but you also have that level of awareness that focusing on celebrating too much can take you away from the path, so you take yourself into inner peace. You don't want to get stuck in some level of pride that doesn't serve you.

This is a state of fulfilment to me—when you feel at ease, your mind is clear and you have a clear understanding of where you are, where you are going, and how much you've already done. This is a state where you feel satisfied and grateful, but you know you are moving forward every day and you have that inner fire, so you wake up every morning inspired.

I personally love that feeling. It is a feeling of trust and gratitude, a feeling of fulfilment. It is a feeling of no regrets.

I speak with people every day, and so many times they ask me if I regret anything. My answer is no. I accept the good and the bad. I accept that I am evolving daily and I'm constantly striving to be a better human being.

Why delve into the past and hang on to unhealthy emotions that hold you back? Ask yourself how to live your life daily in a way you don't regret because you know you did your best up to the level of your awareness, knowledge, and experience. And you know next hour, or tomorrow, you will do better again.

From this space of fulfilment and personal success, write down answers to all the questions we mentioned above:

- How can you live and be better today?
- Who can you help today?
- How can you add value today?
- How can you live daily so you don't regret any action or behaviour?
- How can you evolve even more so you will be better tomorrow?
- What are you here to achieve and contribute to?
- What do you love to do?
- When do you feel the best? If your answer here is "on holidays", please start thinking about what you do differently on your holidays and how to add little holidays to every day.

Start to re-create your life and your lifestyle the way you want and the way you dream.

Now, re-create what you want without using words or limiting beliefs such as, "I can't because of kids/family/time/schedule …" or distracting thoughts such as "I shouldn't/couldn't/wouldn't be able to because …"

I want you to write down on paper everything you want if anything were possible and money, time, or environment were not playing a role or influencing you. This creation or visualisation of what you want is a very important step because, as a leader, you have to be able to imagine where your team is heading before they see it.

That is your authentic goal or vision. Start moving towards it.

Values can also help you to create your vision or understand who and what you truly are.

Values

Values are like a compass. Values are the operating philosophies or principles that guide you or your organisation's conduct, both within and external to the organisation.

Values work both ways—they can be a guiding principle or compass based on the organisation or team's vision and mission, or they can help you find out what you really like and help you create your vision.

So, for team purposes, if mission statements tell you what you're about right now, and vision statements tell you where you're aspiring to be, the core value is to help you get there.

Another way to see it is this—the vision is the 'why'; the mission is the 'what', and the values are the 'how'.

As with everything that is qualitative, we must care about these values translating into real actions and behaviours.

It's one thing to have them published somewhere on the website or on your wall; it's another altogether to have them as part of your performance reviews and day-to-day blueprint of behaviours and attitudes.

Values can be determined in a few ways. Let's have a look at our current and aspirational values by using the exercise below.

Values determination from our session

Your priorities are also known as your **values**. Core values. These are your priorities—aspects of your life you believe are important. Those priorities drive you, consciously and subconsciously.

What you believe is good and bad, what motivates you, how you make decisions, how you allocate your money and time—that is your emotional compass, invisible forces that push you to a destination where you are sailing.

We recognise three types of values. Values of origin, which we learn from our family and friends. We don't think about those values, but they direct and guide our lives. We need to foster awareness of them. After that, we have **current values**, and we can find out easily what those values are based on our results in life, relationships, or work. They are a reflection of our results and life. The most important type of values for us are our **aspirational values**. We can re-create the set of values for us or for our team the way they will guide us, influence us and our behaviours, and move us towards positive and desired results.

Action: Answer those questions for the values determination:

Step 1: Current values—Answer the following questions:

Express values that you live now, not what you want in future. Be honest with yourself. What values you are living is a pretty hard question. What helps my clients the most is to ask:

What is important to you? What do you value about your life, attitude, or behaviour? What do you value from a personality perspective? What do you value right now based on the results you are getting right now?

_____

_____

_____

_____

Step 2: Aspirational values—Answer the following questions:

Express values that you need to integrate and demonstrate daily to achieve what you want. Start with the outcome.

What do you want to achieve? What is the outcome you want to see? It can be your personal goal or your personal values. What is the feeling you want to experience daily? It can be a culture you want to see for the team or organisational values. Please, before you start to determine your organisational values, determine and describe the culture you want to see and experience. The word *experience* is important here:

_____

_____

_____

Aspirational values: Based on the outcome you want, what values do you need to demonstrate? List at least ten values.

_____

_____

Step 3: Numbering—create a hierarchy of values.

Once you've got your values down on paper, number them in order from most important to least important. Don't over analyse your answer. Trust your unconscious mind with whatever answer comes up.

If you find yourself saying, "They are all important to me," just remember to trust your unconscious mind and number them according to what feels most important. Do this task quickly, or it may become confusing.

1. _____
2. _____
3. _____
4. _____
5. _____
6. _____
7. _____

8. _____

9. _____

10._____

Values help you to understand who you are. You can ask questions like, how do you spend money, what do you buy without regret or feeling guilty? What do you see around you? What do you like to keep, collect, or display, maybe on your wall or on the shelves or around you? What is your predominant mood? What is your predominant thought of the day? What is the one thing you always wanted, a kind of long-term goal that is always in your head?

These questions can help you to see who you are and what your values are to guide you to your authentic self.

Attitudes

Self

Having a goal and willingness to achieve it will bring success to every human being. The trouble with an unsuccessful person is that they are not willing to pay the price. Willingness to make any sacrifice to achieve what you want brings real success. The one who only has a goal stays only in a realm of dreams. The person who sees opportunities instead of excuses will succeed. The question to ask here is what the predominant attitude in your mind is. Is it determination to not do certain things or determination to do everything that is required? Is it that your mind is focused on fears of failures and obstacles, or is your mind focused on certainty, on success? Can you visualise what your success looks like? Can you feel it? Can you learn certainty even before you achieve it? If your mind has more fear than faith or belief that this is possible, you will fail. Your attitude determines what will or won't happen for you. If your self-talk and beliefs are destructive, your life will be destructive.

One of my clients' knowledge, drive, and willingness were all amazing, and I couldn't believe he was not as successful as he could be. Something was missing to achieve his highest potential. After working together for the first few weeks, I saw it clearly. There was this massive fault and obstacle that was holding success away from him: judgement of successful people and himself. He was expressing anger, judgement, and suspicion of successful people. It was resentment of his disappointed ego. If you call every successful person a cheater, liar, or unfair, wake up to yourself. I told him to look at this from a different perspective. You only judge others by yourself. What does that mean? If you judge people because they are rich, wealthy, or achieved a lot and you think they are bad people because the only way to the top is to betray someone on the way, or you call them selfish or insincere, it means you are not healed or you see your own faults. It means that, in their situation, you would be selfish or a bad person, or you lack sincerity and honesty. This judgement comes from wounds or fears. We unlocked his old wounds and fears and started to reprogram his mind and his old mood of criticising and judging. In a few days, a week after our session, he got a massive offer from another company to become their CEO with a doubled salary.

Master your mind and attitude so you can become successful and achieve what you want. If you are a leader, think about how easily you can limit the success of your team with this type of attitude.

Leadership

In the realm of our quality of environment, attitude emerges as the defining truth that colours how we think as a collective, how we perceive tasks at hand, those pending, and the potential endeavours awaiting. It's the subtle cadence of inquiry: how does one approach the uncharted, the less inviting, the untravelled?

In those moments when duty calls and the terrain is less than inviting, keen eyes observe. Who steps forth? What melody does their attitude hum? In such moments, the soul speaks volumes.

Yet when the tempests from realms beyond our sway surge forth, how do we stand our ground? Do we lament? Do we wait for the tempest to subside, hoping to remain untouched? Do we offer our aid, albeit half-heartedly, or do we forge ahead, seeking out ways to be of service both to ourselves and others?

During moments of abundance and ease, our attitude is a steadfast companion, reliable yet unsurprising. But it's in the crucible of adversity that the true mettle of our attitude is forged.

Attitude is the very texture of our approach, a prism of qualities to seek:

- Proactive, not reactive

- Taking initiative, not being complacent
- Enthusiasm, not apathy
- Willingness, not reluctance
- Can-do, not apprehensive
- Tenacious, not faltering
- Disciplined, not wavering
- Self-motivated, needing no prodding
- Truthful, speaking as it is
- Perceiving reality as it stands, with no embellishments or diminishments
- Upholding standards in your absence
- Anticipating others to stand firm in their resolve
- Unyielding, unwavering in principles.

These are not just characteristics; they are the essence of a transformative attitude that not only navigates but thrives amidst the ebb and flow of life's currents.

Chapter 5

Emotional Evolution

Knowing ourselves and our emotional blueprint is going to help us to handle every situation, and being aware of where we are in our journey helps us to grow to the next level because we are ongoing evolving, shaping, and growing beings. To improve our emotional intelligence and become emotionally fit, we must understand basic programming, how we create our emotions and feelings at the first stage, and how we can learn to respond instead of react.

I love to draw the simple model of thinking, emotions, and actions and how those communicate and interact as patterns we create.

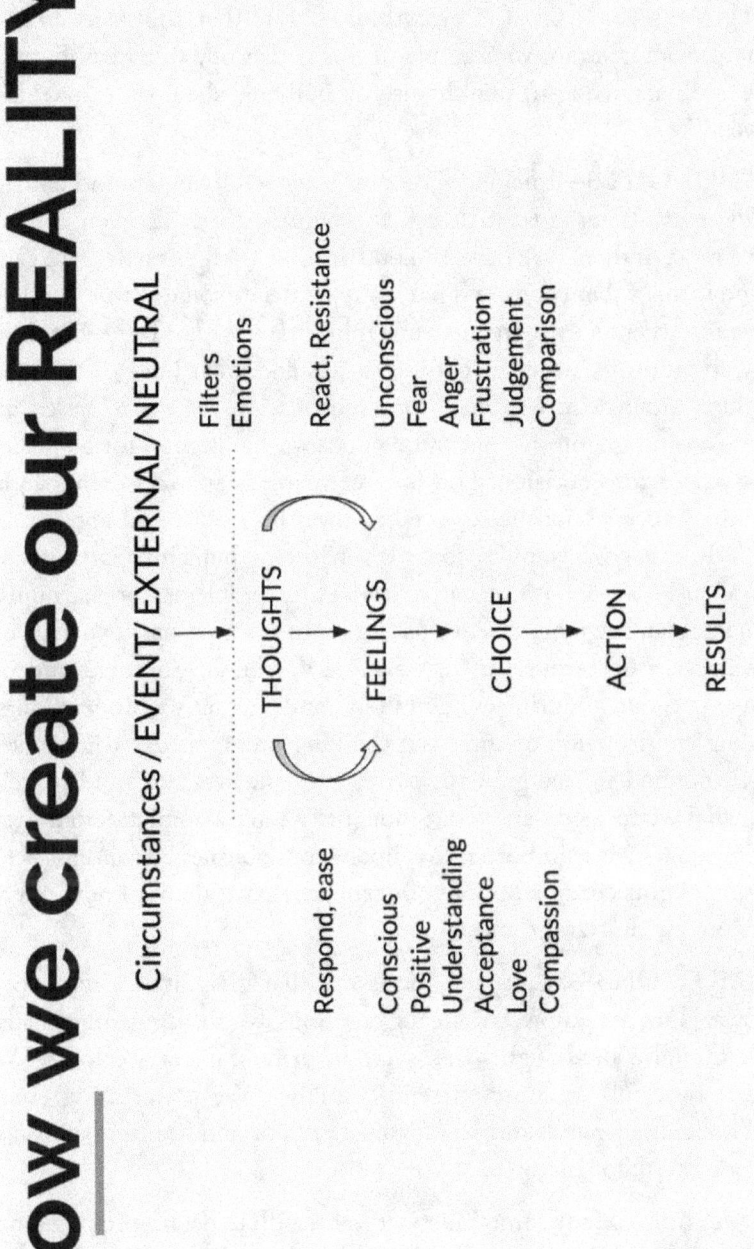

NEUTRAL EVENT—This is anything we see around us or any circumstance we find ourselves in. Every event is neutral until we give it meaning. We give meaning to everything. Before that, things mean nothing and they are all neutral. An example of this is that one thing can bother you, but the next person doesn't find themselves bothered about the same thing and may even like it.

THOUGHTS—Imagine thoughts as clouds flying around and, at any time, there are thousands of thoughts around without us even consciously noticing most of them. We have 100,000 or more thoughts a day. We can't pay attention to all of them at once. That's why we delete some of them and distort or generalise them so we organise our minds day-to-day. But what thoughts we pay attention to, what we choose to see, and what kind of thoughts we see coming around are written in our subconscious program. Based on our subconscious programming, our mind chooses what is good for us without us making a conscious decision. This is how we are as an average human being. By training our consciousness, we take power over our mind and we decide, consciously, what we want to focus on. Most of humanity is programmed subconsciously to choose negative thoughts, problems, or harmful self-judgemental language because we have a lot of negative past experiences and we see it every day around us or on the TV. The environment and people around us program us during our childhood, and later on, we program ourselves by finding confirmation of these old thinking programs. As you can see, we make a voice and we can gain our power over our lives back and consciously decide what we focus on and what thoughts we allow to dictate our lives. It's your choice. Why is it important to choose consciousness? Conscious choice? Because thoughts create emotions. Our mood. As we already know, our mood dictates our circumstances and results.

EMOTIONS—So, if your life is not that great, it is a result of your emotions. Now, we know we create emotions by focusing on negative or positive thoughts or thoughts that serve us or do a disservice to us. We can call it "resourceful" or "unresourceful" thinking. We are creating emotions daily. Think about one common language pattern and limiting subconscious thinking pattern; for example:

Every time you say something you want, wish to do, have, or become, you end by saying **but**. **But** it is a very dangerous word. It cancels everything you said beforehand. "I like your T-shirt, **but** it wouldn't suit me. I want to be your friend, **but** I don't have enough time for relationships." Can you see how **but** can easily influence what you say? Because what matters to our emotions and the emotions of others is how we say it. You program yourself deeper every day when you are telling yourself all the lies about your dream or desired results: **but** I don't have time, **but** I don't have enough money to start or do it, **but** I don't know anyone who can help, and so on. These kinds of thoughts create disappointment, distrust of yourself, low self-esteem, and a feeling that you can't make it. Most of the time, this program is created by our language. We say things like, "I want to do it ... **but** ... I don't have time, power, or connections." We are making our own problems and our own insecurities ourselves. By using negative language, we are disregarding our wishes and wants in our minds, and so it becomes our reality.

Now, the good news is that you can change it. You can reprogram your mind and yourself today. You can become successful in this minute because when you change your predominant mood and emotions based on your thoughts. It's only a question of time until you get what you want. You need to first become the person you want to be, then you will create what you want.

ACTIONS—Now, when we have finally programmed our new mind and consciously approach the world from better moods, emotions, and thinking patterns, we take action aligned with this new self. We know there is no **but**. We know now that taking action is as important as setting up your mind and emotional state. Now, you are prepared to act. But what action needs to be taken? Well, exactly the action that you wish for yourself. Do you want to be happy? It's time to act and make someone else happy today. Make someone else's day better. Do you want to be rich and have more money? Give money today. Give away at least 10% of your income or what you have. First, you need to give. This is the golden rule for **action**. First, give what you want for yourself. Stop giving what you don't wish for yourself. Do as you wish others to do for you. Do you want help? Help someone else today.

Be resourceful and creative. Be open to try things and watch what happens next. Don't create attachments to your goals or your actions. Don't think about it this way: "Now that I've given, I need to get." No!

Give, give, give, and you'll get, and so continue giving to not break the cycle. This is generosity. If you want to meet more generous people, more kind people, you must be that first.

There is abundance and kindness, there is love and generosity, so create it. Be it.

Don't hurt people with your actions. Do good always with intentions to do good.

RESULTS—I feel like I don't need to even talk about results. Results and our circumstances are direct reflections of all the above—our thoughts, emotions, and actions. I'm sure you can see it now. If you project jealousy onto the world, the world will give it back to you in the form of disappointment, hurt, or bad news. If you wish someone bad, the world will give it to you back in various forms. It can be injury, bad luck, loss. If you wish for someone to fail, you will fail. I'm sure you get the picture. But the question, then, is why don't you have what you want yet? Or why are you not feeling happy, healthy, and successful yet?

Look at your results today, now. What do you have? What do you create? Take it as a reflection on your thoughts, emotions, and behaviours. Adjust your mind, attitude, and emotional state to create better outcomes.

Ultimate transformation is a journey of discovery. What I found by working with thousands of C-suite level leaders and my team is that emotions or moods are the guiding hand to our results. Emotions or moods, even those deep down we don't pay attention to, are very important.

Those are the guiding principles we need to master. Emotions are solutions, but what are the predominant emotions we need to master to achieve what we want? Or what we *truly* want?

I will go through the major steps of emotional evolution and transformation to better results, which are mastering awareness, self-awareness, courage, confidence, and purpose.

Stage 1: Awareness

There can be no change without awareness. By awareness, I mean understanding your environment and seeing where you are, reflecting on a situation, person, or feeling with openness and curiosity. A new level of awareness emerges when you ask questions like "What is it about this that I'm not seeing yet?", "What is it about this person that I'm reacting to?", and "What is it about me?"

You can develop awareness in a number of ways. We will use a few tools to assess your environment and yourself. One of them is eDISC behavioural profiling, which truly helps to recognise the basics of behaviours and the nature of some needs. We will also talk about human needs. We will use feedback and power questions. We are going to develop a few frameworks and thinking models to help you understand yourself and others on a deeper level.

This is only the first step, and here your task is to bring awareness to you, your emotions, and your environment and be aware that you are interacting and connecting with your environment. Everything is interconnected and sees and observes all that is present.

After this, the next stage to move to if you want to make change is choosing to observe it deeper and observe how it influences you and others.

Stage 2: Self-Awareness

Self-awareness is the ability to focus on yourself and how your actions, thoughts, or emotions do or don't align with your internal standards. If you're highly self-aware, you can objectively evaluate yourself, manage your emotions, align your behaviour with your values, and understand correctly how others perceive you.

When we are self-aware, we are able to recognise our strengths and weaknesses. This knowledge helps us to set goals for ourselves. We know where we have room to grow, and that's a good thing! Our strengths help us feel confident in our ability to improve on our weaknesses.

This part is going to be focused on developing a clear understanding of who we are, who we want to be as a leader, what our strengths are, and what our preferred thinking and behavioural patterns are.

Stage 3: Courage

A lot of people think that conscious living and leading is only being self-aware. The problem is that being self-aware is a great start, but it doesn't bring any fruit and doesn't serve others if we don't act on it effectively.

Let's dive deeper into this. Everything starts with a psychological state. I can share a few stories I hear every day. I will share a recent example from a meeting last week.

Her story

I recently met an incredible woman at a charming Italian restaurant, one of my favourite spots in Brisbane. This place has been around for over 50 years, run by a lovely Italian family, and they serve the most delicious food while also offering some of the best European products. It's a cosy place that feels like home, and every visit is a treat.

We met because a mutual friend introduced us, and I said yes to catching up over coffee. I'm always open to meeting new people—there's something beautiful about learning someone's story, and that day was no different.

She's a talented author and facilitator, highly skilled in her field, but at the time, she was navigating some heavy personal challenges. She was going through a difficult divorce, and the emotional toll from years of abuse at home had started to reflect in her business. Cash flow became tight, and more deeply, she found herself grappling with feelings of unworthiness.

There's often a direct link between cash flow and self-worth—when you feel undeserving, it shows up in your financial life, too.

Despite her expertise, her years of emotional and verbal abuse had chipped away at her confidence and self-belief. Over two decades of being put down by her husband left her with deeply ingrained limiting beliefs about herself—her worth, her abilities, and her potential. It was as if her subconscious had absorbed the idea that she wasn't worthy of success, love, or abundance.

Her outer reality began to mirror those inner beliefs. She kept encountering situations that confirmed her fears—she wasn't enough, and she saw evidence of that everywhere. It was almost as if she unconsciously sought out moments that reinforced this painful narrative.

A moment during our coffee perfectly highlighted this.

We were sitting at the table, sipping our coffees and enjoying the peaceful atmosphere. I noticed her glancing around the restaurant at the staff. After a moment, she leaned in and said, "I think the waitress isn't happy with us because we only ordered coffee." I let the comment slide at first, not wanting to interrupt her thoughts.

But then she mentioned it again—and again. By the third time, she nervously pointed out that maybe we had been sitting there too long without ordering food, convinced the staff were giving us rude looks.

I had to pause and gently say something. This was an opportunity for her to see what was happening.

I love this restaurant. I've been coming here for years and never once felt unwelcome or like I wasn't a valuable customer. I saw smiles all around, warm service, and the typical charm of European hospitality. To me, it felt like being part of a family. But to her, it felt different.

She was so stressed and anxious about overstaying with just a coffee that it seemed almost ridiculous. The difference in our experiences was striking.

It wasn't the restaurant or the staff—it was her belief that she wasn't worthy of simply sitting there and enjoying the moment.

That realisation opened the door to a deeper conversation. It unlocked a new level of awareness about how she was living and how these subconscious patterns played out in everyday life. It wasn't just about coffee; it was about how she carried that sense of unworthiness into so many spaces.

But that day, with a little shift in perspective, something began to change.

Now, awareness is a great start, but she didn't stop there. She took action and began shifting her views on herself and her relationship with wealth. She found the courage to look inward, recognising these patterns in her daily life. From that point forward, she committed to taking opposite actions—correcting her responses and rewriting the narrative she had been living.

Courage is taking action despite old limitations and fears and installing a new, better belief. Action with faith. As an example here, the courage would be starting the day with a question: "What if I feel confident and believe I can do everything?" What would I be? What would I do today, right now, if I fully believe in myself and I know I am enough and worth it?"

From these questions, new types of actions and behaviours come to your mind. Take that as a guide and do it. Step into new beliefs and make decisions based on that.

Stage 4: Confidence

In the next stage, after taking new actions and making new decisions based on positive beliefs and faith, you are starting to build a psychology of confidence. Why do you think that? Well, as we know by now, thoughts create our feelings. Thinking creates emotions and, based on emotions, we act and create results. When we react to negative emotions, we live in a lack mindset, with daily fear and worries about the future. So our predominant feeling or mood is to feel like we always need to get something instead of give. Then our decisions, language, and behaviours will display these thoughts and emotions, so you will be seen as someone who is always trying to get something. You won't be an attractive companion for others, and there will be no-one who will be willing to help you because you have this energy and feeling around you like you want to only get. People feel each other. We are energetic beings. This is happening from our subconscious program and subconscious mind. If you change your psychology and your thoughts from lack to abundance, you feel more at ease and you live in gratitude. You will act differently and you will make other people around you feel great so you will build a network of people who feel the same and want to help each other. You won't need to ask for anything. You will attract that and get what you want just by being in a positive vibration, mindset, and emotions.

Changing your psychology is the most important part of your success.

You can gain confidence by ongoing mind training, learning, and becoming great in what you do and sharing and practising your knowledge so it becomes wisdom and skill. But most importantly, it all starts with your predominant thoughts and emotions. When you act from an abundant mind, you will finally see that life is happening *for* you, not *to* you. From that space and experience of life, you will gain more confidence every day.

Stage 5: Purpose

When you become more confident, you will start to see openings in your life's journey to refocus more on meaning. You realise that meaning is a real success. Doing something meaningful, contributing more, and being generous with your time, thoughts, and presence will bring others more success and more fulfilment to you.

This stage is when we start to focus on what we truly love, what our passion is, and what we want to create—how we want to add value and contribute to this world and people. You can only develop or arrive at this stage after you understand consciousness and understand that life is happening for you and that you are a powerful creator of every circumstance after you connect within and understand who you truly are. Authenticity and confidence will create a path for you to fully express yourself. Remember, the world needs you, and you have been preparing for your contribution all your life.

Life is a journey, and all the lessons you need to learn are preparing you for this stage where you can contribute more.

Don't forget to notice you are living in all five stages; sometimes you can experience them all in one day. This is more about the psychological stage, not really the life journey that happens at a certain age.

Yes, we naturally start at the beginning and build awareness over our lifetime. When we are more mature, we move more into meaning, but it doesn't mean we are not living a meaningful life or not doing what we love at any stage. That doesn't mean you are not contributing to life or people. You are naturally a contributor. Every day, you are influencing people around you, and if you put more focus, confidence, and awareness into this, you will later realise how you can contribute in a more effective way.

Moving to a higher state of decision-making

This is a powerful model we've been using to help our clients work through the process of change. It's called the Awareness-Acceptance-Action Model, and it's a framework or continuum with three stages. Moving through each stage will help you experience a different response in any given situation so that you can create real change. Now we will describe a more practical method to move from one stage to another.

Stage 1: Awarenes

You learn enough about awareness and self-awareness. You can now observe your emotions and thoughts daily and you are becoming a conscious human being who knows what's going on inside. You step into a state where you can recognise your triggers—thoughts that trigger particular emotions and reactions.

Stage 2: Acceptance

Most people, when they observe their triggers, become angry with themselves and start fighting those emotions and triggers. They start being irritated or angry with themselves or with this part of themselves. We can call it the dark side, the side they don't like. They fight it, resist it, and try to stop it.

But this becomes a very powerful energy and they accidentally make their dark side even more powerful because they are feeding it with energy and focus.

But acceptance is about having dark and light sides in us and accepting they all have their own role in our life and they are needed.

There will be no black without white. There will be no desire for peace without knowing the war.

This is about accepting who you are at that moment. For example: you've lost your cool—it's not ideal, but you're aware of it and you're accepting of it without resisting that it's happening. This is a key point because, if you experience resistance, it's a sign that you're not aligned. It's only when you can accept where you are right now that you create alignment with your mind, body, and emotions. And it's only then you can move forward into action.

When you refuse to accept where you are right now—and recognise that your current reality is a result of your own actions and choices—it's often because you're stuck in a victim mindset or living in denial. You might be afraid to look inward and face the truth, fearing that it could bring discomfort or pain.

In this state, you can't move forward, grow, or break through. You remain stuck in a cycle of victimhood.

It's crucial to remember that acceptance is the key to breaking free. Acceptance doesn't mean you approve of the situation or passively resign yourself to it. It means acknowledging where you are so you can learn from it and begin to change. The feeling of being stuck often comes with a lesson—so lean into it, accept it, and allow yourself to grow.

However, there's another form of acceptance that can also keep people stuck. This happens when someone says, "This is just who I am, and there's nothing I can do about it." In this case, acceptance becomes an excuse, a way to avoid growth or responsibility.

Many people use blame as a defence mechanism to protect themselves. By blaming others for their circumstances, they temporarily feel better, convincing themselves that their struggles are someone else's fault. This provides a sense of relief, but it keeps them from developing emotional fitness.

Why does this happen? Blame releases tension in the body and creates a false sense of control. Psychologically, it feels like action—but in reality, it's like standing in place, shifting from one foot to the other without ever moving forward.

True progress begins when you stop blaming and start taking ownership. Acceptance, paired with action, leads to transformation.

Stage 3: Action

Nothing happens until something moves.

-Anonymous

When we move into action, we gather information that leads us down another path and ultimately through the situation, feeling, or event. If we jump into action in a state of resistance while operating predominantly from the amygdala or fight-or-flight mode or we are in misalignment with our authentic self, it will feel like an uphill struggle. However, if we've been through a process of understanding, reflection, asking questions, and accepting what is and then moving into action, we've built energy around it. With momentum on your side, the shift is not so hard. Yes, it might still be challenging, but the magic of this three-stage framework is that it brings the mind, body, and emotions together to move along the **path of least resistance.**

So, before jumping into action, ask yourself the following questions

- What awareness do I have around the issue?
- Where can I feel the resistance, and what I am resistant to?
- How do I feel about moving into action?
- Does it feel good, or do I feel like I have to do it?
- Does my action create what I want for someone else?
- Am I doing good? Am I being generous?

Asking yourself just these questions will give you clarity around whether it's the right action for you.

I also recommend you start using the word "feel". Even for those who are predominantly "thinkers", using the word "feel" will open up elements in your psyche that you might not have tapped into before. Feeling is our guidance system. Just think about any purchase you made in the past few weeks. How do you think you are making buying decisions?

By emotions of course, by feelings.

How do you think you choose friends? You feel good with them right?

Feel into the situation, event, or person.

What does it bring up in you? There may be a feeling that's telling you something is unresolved or that's reminding you of something you need to look out for. If you feel uncomfortable, it's for a reason.

Maybe even conversations about feelings make you uncomfortable. Maybe you don't truly know how you feel right now. If this is true, that doesn't mean you don't feel or that something is wrong with you. It means you haven't developed the emotional language yet because it wasn't very common in your environment to talk about feelings. Maybe you disconnected from yourself a little bit, but that is okay. We are building up connections throughout this book, and I can say you are going to be okay and connected within if you choose.

Sometimes you don't need to find out exactly what the reason is—it's enough to know that you feel uncomfortable, which begs the question: **"What can I do to feel more comfortable expressing my emotions or pausing to look within so I see what I feel?"** or **"What can I do about this situation, event, or person?"**

If you're feeling particularly stuck or frustrated, try out some of these questions about developing awareness:

- What am I actually feeling right now?
- What is this situation or person telling me about myself?
- What is good about this situation that I don't yet understand?

If you feel very strong negative emotions, I suggest you use the breathing exercises below or try to take yourself to a time when you felt great, satisfied, or grateful in the past and connect with those feelings. Feel what you experienced then.

The quickest way to accept something is to breathe. It releases tension. Breath is your power; it is a life force. Breathing techniques will help you to resolve a lot of internal tension.

You can use box breathing. This is used in military training to improve emotional response and take people out of fight-or-flight mode. It helps to lower cortisol levels and stress so the person can respond effectively and appropriately.

Miracles through breathing

> *An intelligent person is not closed-minded. He does not behave like an ostrich burying his head in the ground, trying to avoid new ideas and developments.*
>
> *An intelligent person is not gullible. He does not accept ideas blindly. He studies and digests them thoroughly, then evaluates them against his reason; he tests these new ideas and developments through experiments and his experiences. An intelligent person studies these ideas with a clear objective mind.*
>
> —Master Choa Kok Sui, *Miracles Through Pranic Healing*

When I attended a pranic healing course and started practising Master Choa Kok Sui's teachings, I had doubts—too many doubts. I was telling myself it couldn't work. It was too much for an analytical and pragmatic mind. But with time and practice, you realise slowly that all you thought, and all logic, can be challenged. So, I started to look at the results and asked myself why do we doubt and resent some ideas? Because they are outside our own map of realities and possibilities. Remember, your map is not a territory. It is only your one map of possible thoughts and realities you once decided to believe. And maybe you created this map when you were six or eight years old. Is it possible this map stopped expanding and started shrinking?

Exploring the territory beyond the map

In the theme of our subconscious minds, there exists a concept that states, "The map is not the territory." This profound idea suggests that our perceptions, beliefs, and understanding of the world around us, represented by our mental maps, are not the same as the reality they attempt to depict. Instead, they are subjective interpretations coloured by our experiences, memories, values, and beliefs.

However, within the vast expanse of our subconscious there often lie hidden territories that remain unexplored and untouched by the light of conscious awareness. These territories are the repositories of our deepest fears, insecurities, and limiting beliefs, shaped by past traumas, negative experiences, and societal conditioning.

When we allow these limiting beliefs to dictate our thoughts, actions, and choices, we inadvertently confine ourselves within the boundaries of our mental maps, restricting our potential and limiting our possibilities. We become prisoners of our own perceptions, unable to see beyond the confines of our self-imposed limitations.

We miss out on a lot of things if we stay stuck in our map without seeing what is beyond the boundaries.

We may miss out on some opportunities for growth. By transcending our limiting beliefs, we open ourselves up to a world of endless possibilities and opportunities for growth, learning, and self-discovery. We become more adaptable, resilient, and open-minded, ready to embrace new experiences and challenges.

Breaking free from the shackles of limiting beliefs allows us to tap into our true potential and live authentically. We experience a deeper sense of fulfilment, purpose, and joy as we align our actions with our values and pursue our passions without fear or hesitation.

Limiting beliefs often sabotage our relationships by fuelling insecurities, distrust, and miscommunication. By expanding our map, we cultivate healthier, more fulfilling relationships built on trust, empathy, and mutual respect.

When we challenge our limiting beliefs and step outside our comfort zones, we unlock new pathways to success, achievement, and personal mastery. We become more resilient in the face of setbacks, more creative in problem-solving, and more determined in pursuing our goals. By transforming our own limiting beliefs, we become more empathetic, compassionate, and understanding towards others. We forge deeper connections and foster a sense of belonging within our friends, families, or community.

To me, expanding our map beyond the territory of our limiting beliefs, thoughts, or memories is not merely an act of self-discovery but a journey towards greater freedom, fulfilment, and authenticity. It is a testament to the resilience of the human spirit and the boundless potential that lies within each and every one of us, waiting to be unleashed.

One of the greatest tools to unleash our full potential and try to stop our subconscious limiting mind from directing our life is breathing or changing our physical state or mood.

Breathing techniques are the fastest way to transformation and freedom.

But how to breathe?

Breathing, often overlooked as a mundane and automatic bodily function, holds remarkable power when utilised intentionally. The process of breathing involves the exchange of oxygen and carbon dioxide in the body, crucial for sustaining life. However, beyond its basic physiological function, breathing deeply and consciously can profoundly impact our physical, mental, and emotional wellbeing, facilitating transformation on various levels. Breathing techniques definitely changed my life and helped me to move away from fear, anxiety, and stress to living in peace and ease.

The most common physiological effects of intentional breathing are lowering stress levels, detoxification, and the oxygenation of cells.

Deep breathing techniques, such as diaphragmatic breathing or belly breathing, facilitate the intake of oxygen into the bloodstream. This oxygen-rich blood is then circulated throughout the body, nourishing cells, organs, and tissues and supporting optimal bodily function. Deep breathing activates the parasympathetic nervous system, often referred to as the "rest and digest" system. This activation triggers a relaxation response, lowering heart rate, blood pressure, and cortisol levels, thereby reducing stress and promoting a state of calmness and relaxation. Deep breathing enhances the efficiency of the lymphatic system, which is responsible for removing toxins and waste products from the body. By promoting lymphatic drainage, breathing supports detoxification processes, aiding in the elimination of metabolic waste and promoting overall health and vitality.

There is so much more. Intentional or conscious breathing has an impact on your nervous system, too. Breathing serves as a bridge between the autonomic nervous system's two branches: the sympathetic and parasympathetic nervous systems. By modulating our breath, we can influence the balance between these two systems, shifting from a state of stress and arousal to one of relaxation and calmness.

Deep, diaphragmatic breathing stimulates the vagus nerve, a key component of the parasympathetic nervous system. Enhanced vagal tone is associated with improved mood, reduced inflammation, and enhanced resilience to stress, promoting overall wellbeing and emotional stability.

Conscious breathing cultivates mindfulness and awareness of the present moment, fostering a deeper connection between mind and body. I love to practise even a few seconds a day while focusing on the movement of my belly, clearing my mind of thoughts wandering elsewhere. This heightened awareness allows me to observe and regulate my thoughts, emotions, and physical sensations, building greater self-awareness and emotional intelligence.

Deep breathing techniques help regulate emotions by activating brain regions associated with emotional processing and regulation, such as the prefrontal cortex and amygdala. By calming the mind and body, breathing facilitates emotional balance and helps you to navigate challenging situations with greater ease and access to intellect.

After a while of practising mindful breathing, I felt like I had the innate potential for healing, growth, and self-discovery, paving the way for my own personal transformation.

Now, I'm sharing this as the simplest technique you can start without needing any ongoing assistance or a coach.

I will share a few techniques that my clients and myself love to use.

Box breathing

Always focus on breathing through your lungs and belly. Take a deep slow breath a few times and start counting:

Step 1: Breathe in, counting slowly to four. Feel the air enter your lungs.

Step 2: Hold your breath for six seconds. Try to avoid inhaling or exhaling for six seconds.

Step 3: Slowly exhale through your mouth for six seconds.

Step 4: Repeat steps 1 to 3 until you feel re-centred.

If it gets uncomfortable when you're in the acceptance phase, try to stay open to that. From that discomfort, you can move into action, asking yourself, "Do I want to do something about it? Yes, I do."

When moving into action, take the next most logical step and the path of least resistance. Now when you calm yourself and lower your stress, you are able to use all the powerful parts of your brain to connect within and make decisions about your actions. Try to avoid taking action in a state of overwhelm, stress, doubt, or fear.

Pranic breathing for healing and energy

What is prana? Pranayama is the practice of breath regulation. It's a main component of yoga, an exercise for physical and mental wellness. In Sanskrit, *prana* means "life energy" and *yama* means "control". Basically, controlled breathing.

Pranic breathing is a yogic practice that invigorates the body and mind, fostering strength, vitality, and inner balance. Through pranic breathing, you will tap into the abundant life force energy known as prana and absorb its rejuvenating essence.

This technique involves various breathing patterns designed to optimise the intake and circulation of prana throughout the body:

- **Deep breathing with empty retention.** Inhale deeply, hold the breath, exhale completely, and hold again, repeating this cycle seven times. This rhythmic pattern enhances pranic absorption and energises the body.
- **6-3-6-3 breathing.** Inhale for six counts, hold the breath for three counts, exhale for six counts, and hold again for three counts, repeating the sequence seven times. This structured breathing pattern balances energy flow and promotes mental clarity.

Practising these physical and pranic breathing exercises each morning offers a lot of healing benefits. It helps maintain physical health, enhance mental flexibility, and sharpen focus. Moreover, they possess a revitalising effect, cleansing the chakras, your energy centres, and meridians of stagnant or negative energies.

Incorporating pranic breathing into your daily routine empowers you to cultivate a harmonious connection between body, mind, and spirit, fostering overall wellbeing and vitality.

Thoughts and emotional flexibility

Our thoughts, being the architects of our reality, hold incredible power in shaping how we perceive and experience the world around us. They act as the lens through which we view our existence, colour our emotions, and influence our actions. Moreover, they become the mirror reflecting the depths of our soul, laying bare the essence of our being.

Each living soul embarks on a profoundly individual journey, seeking and experiencing a unique path through life, which explains why all humans perceive and interpret reality differently. Our thoughts become the palette with which we paint our world, splashing it with colours of our beliefs, experiences, and emotions. Thus, our inner dialogue profoundly impacts the external landscapes we navigate daily.

The influence of our subconscious mind on our circumstances is often described with an iceberg analogy, where only a small portion is visible above the water while the majority remains hidden beneath. In this analogy, the iceberg represents the mind, with the visible tip representing the conscious mind, and the submerged part symbolising the subconscious mind.

Imagine the conscious mind as the 10% that is above the water, easily seen and recognised. This is the part of our mind that deals with logical thinking, reasoning, and decision-making on a day-to-day basis. It's what we are aware of in our thoughts and actions daily.

Now, let's talk about the hidden 90%, which is the subconscious mind beneath the surface. This part of the mind stores memories, emotions, beliefs, and automatic responses. It also stores thought processes based on our memories, fears, and internal beliefs that are not yet known on the surface level. They are all hidden, and so many times we don't have any awareness of those beliefs guiding our lives.

It plays a crucial role in shaping our behaviour, reactions, and overall perception of the world. Many of our habits, fears, and patterns are deeply rooted in the subconscious.

If someone is struggling with slow business growth, stress, or burnout, the underlying causes often reside in the subconscious mind. Negative beliefs, self-sabotaging thoughts, or past experiences can influence your decisions and actions without conscious awareness.

The process of understanding and transforming the subconscious is crucial for personal and professional development and also for your happiness and fulfilment. Techniques such as mindfulness, meditation, and coaching, especially those inspired by the principles of ontological coaching, neuroscience, or the CEB method, can help you tap into and reshape your subconscious beliefs. This, in turn, can lead to a positive shift in mindset, improved decision-making, and ultimately, more significant success and wellbeing.

Acknowledging the power of the subconscious mind, represented by the submerged portion of the iceberg, is key to creating lasting change and achieving a state of ease, inner peace, happiness, and effectiveness in both personal and professional aspects of life.

In the teachings of Sydney Banks, the three principles of mind, consciousness, and thought emerge as foundational cornerstones of psychological functioning, and this is similar to the teachings of other masters such as Michael Singer or yogis such as Yogananda. These elements are inseparable and interwoven, providing us with the necessary tools to make sense of our existence and respond to the stimuli we encounter.

It shows us those three elements create our circumstances and reality. There is one great example when you think about one person that really irritates you or makes you angry. When you ask your friend what they think about that person or how they feel about them or their behaviour, they will answer something like "I don't even notice." So, we have proof every day that nothing and no-one can make us feel something or make us angry or frustrated—only we make ourselves angry and bothered about something. We create all those emotions and feelings.

Mind, the wellspring of our thoughts and consciousness, births the creative force within us. It bestows upon us the divine gift of thought, empowering us to direct our journey through life.

This master key unlocks the door to the realm of reality for all living beings, bridging the gap between the spiritual and material worlds.

Within the concept of thought, the dynamic interplay of positivity and negativity unfolds, each carrying profound implications for our mental and emotional wellbeing. When we embrace positive thoughts, we cultivate a healthy and stable mind, leading us on a path to greater happiness and fulfilment. Optimism acts as a spiritual quality and a guiding light, illuminating our way through the darkest of times.

On the contrary, the grip of pessimism taints our thought system with despair, veiling the true potential of our being. Negative thoughts create a ripple effect, generating negative feelings and behaviours, eventually becoming the seeds of human suffering and illness.

In the concept of thought lies the profound gift of free will and free thought imbuing us with the stamp of individuality. It allows us to shape our perception of life, forging our unique path amidst the vastness of the human experience. Yet, we may find ourselves swimming in negative thought patterns, struggling to break free from the chains of past experiences and memories written in our subconscious mind.

Embracing the wisdom of positive thoughts and transcending the limitations of negative thinking leads us towards unity with that which is good. As the wise proclaim, "I think, therefore, I am," signifying the transformative power of our thoughts to shape our very identity and reality.

On the other hand, the voice of the fool echoes, "I don't think so," suggesting the refusal to embrace the potential for positive change and growth. The dichotomy between the wise and the fool lies in the willingness to cultivate positive thoughts, leading to a life of purpose, fulfilment, and harmony, or to succumb to pessimism and darkness, denying ourselves the brilliance of our own potential.

In the broader landscape of human consciousness, our thoughts serve as the architects of our journey, charting the course of our destiny. By nurturing a mindset of optimism, we open ourselves to the limitless possibilities that life has to offer. In this transformational dance between mind, consciousness, and thought, we wield the creative power to transcend limitations, embrace growth, and forge a reality that aligns with our deepest desires.

There are many major limiting thinking patterns that create negative thoughts, such as judgement of yourself and others and comparison. We like to torture ourselves by comparing ourselves to someone more successful or someone who already achieved what we want without paying attention to reality. So many times we realise too late that the person who we think is so fulfilled and successful is more desperate and is suffering quietly inside than we thought. Also, that person may need our help or attention but instead, we give them a nasty look because we are jealous of or angry with their success. Those limiting thinking patterns cause a lot of bad feelings and bad behaviours, so they are taking us away from success and happiness.

I will give you a few questions that I used to start this journey of consciousness and awareness to create more success, so you can do it every day too.

Ask yourself

EXERCISE THOUGHTS:

1. Start journalling your morning thoughts. What are your first and second thoughts? What are you thinking about first thing in the morning? Don't put any energy into those thoughts for now. Just observe.
2. Take yourself on "judgement watch"; where and when do you judge yourself or others?
3. Where do you compare yourself? Again, observe and don't get into judgement or feeling guilty. Just observe and let it be part of you.

How we create our reality

Your thoughts shape your feelings, and your feelings influence your decisions, actions, and the results you experience. If your thoughts are filled with negativity and resentment, they generate emotions that drain your energy, keeping you stuck in limiting patterns.

But when you shift your thoughts to focus on future visions, dreams, and possibilities, your emotions and energy naturally follow. Positive, inspiring thoughts create feelings of vitality and excitement, fuelling even more expansive and vision-driven ideas.

Where your focus goes, energy flows. By choosing to concentrate on empowering thoughts and uplifting possibilities, you can change not only how you feel but also the energy you bring into each moment. This shift in focus transforms your decisions and ultimately the reality you create.

I've seen this play out firsthand with my clients. I was working with two business partners who were frustrated with each other. One of the owners told me that the other wasn't contributing—he wasn't bringing ideas, solutions, or suggestions and seemed disengaged from the company's growth and direction.

Later, when I spoke to the other partner, a very different story emerged. He explained that he had tried to share his ideas and solutions many times, but they were often disregarded or dismissed. Over time, he felt unheard and unappreciated, so he eventually stopped offering input altogether.

The situation escalated until both partners felt stuck—one believing the other didn't care while the other felt invisible and unvalued.

Eventually, we sat down together, and with me as a mediator, they had an open and honest conversation. What we uncovered was eye-opening. The breakdown wasn't due to a lack of ideas or effort but stemmed from miscommunication driven by each partner's limiting beliefs and self-doubts.

One partner's belief that "my ideas aren't good enough" collided with the other's fear of "I have to do this alone". These subconscious patterns created a reality where neither felt supported, and the business suffered as a result.

By shifting their focus and reframing their thoughts, they began to recognise the value in each other's contributions. This small but powerful change in mindset opened the door to better communication, trust, and collaboration.

The lesson? Our thoughts and beliefs shape not only our internal world but the relationships and environments we engage with. Change your thoughts, and you change your energy. Change your energy, and you shift the outcomes you experience.

Sometimes, we think we know everything, but if we have a look at our thinking, we realise there are so many angles we can see things from. Also, we deliver ideas with different intentions and most of the time our language impacts how our ideas are perceived. We may say one or two words that may trigger the other person. Without awareness, we are always going to create a gap in communication and we almost always fail to negotiate or bring ideas to fruition. The best way is always to start with an acknowledgement of the other person's feelings and emotions and ask a lot of questions before we bring our new idea to the table. My old friend taught me something, and I will never forget it. He said: "Always talk to someone so they feel like your idea was actually their own. If the intention and focus are on the result, who actually cares whose idea it was, right?"

Remember, how we think about our actions, activities, and behaviours creates our reality. Also, our thinking is the cause of our actions, behaviours, and attitudes. Intentions guide our energy and subconscious body language. So, check yourself first before you start a conversation.

This part is really important for emotional intelligence. We are thinking creatures, and if we are now aware of the importance of thoughts, we know based on those we act and create our behaviours. Now we can choose to **respond** or **react**.

A lot of people become subconscious robots after their thirties. We live our lives automatically on autopilot.

Let's journal our emotional intelligence and our emotional response. Let's have a look at what our triggers are and what we can do to improve our emotional intelligence.

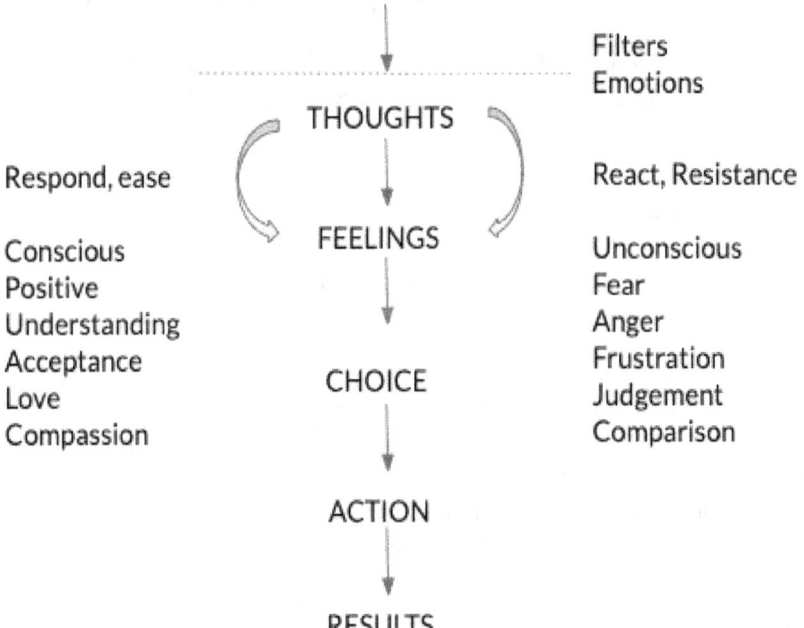

What is emotional intelligence?

Emotional intelligence (otherwise known as emotional quotient or EQ) is the ability to understand, use, and manage your own emotions in positive ways to relieve stress, communicate effectively, empathise with others, overcome challenges, and defuse conflict.

According to Daniel Goleman, an American psychologist who helped to popularise emotional intelligence, there are five key elements to it:

- Self-awareness
- Self-regulation
- Motivation
- Empathy
- Social skills

What do you think it means to be an emotionally fit leader?

Dr Daniel Goleman says that emotional intelligence is measured by the quality of one's relationship with uncertainty. Most people have an addiction to certainty.

How do you behave?

Have you ever been triggered by something or someone? Did the way you react surprise you? We all need to understand we have a shadow and light part of us or the part we don't like and the part we are proud of. Internally, we like and dislike something inside of us. Some attributes, behaviours, attitudes, beliefs. When something external triggers us, usually it's triggering or uncovering the part we don't like about us. The part we don't want to see. We need to embrace both and understand the difference. We need to understand that our good side wouldn't be there without our bad side.

Aspects of ourselves:

- Engage the part of you dislike (shadow) when it's getting hard.
- Embrace fear and uncertainty.
- Bring in self-honesty and observe thoughts.

- Acknowledge your thoughts and choose to let go!
- Integration is a journey of self-trust, self-respect, and self-esteem. Develop a belief in yourself. I build trust so that no matter what happens outside, I trust what comes from inside over the outside. Trust your perception.
- When you put more faith in the outside, the part you dislike is in charge.
- Be loyal to the path you are on. Be loyal to your inside. Listen within.
- When we live in light, we are aligned with our values; we are not living in victimhood or ego.

We need to take life impersonally. Life is not personal. We are here to resolve *thinking* that creates a problem, not a problem. We are here to learn how we create our lives or make decisions. Feelings and emotions are something you *have*, not something you *are*. The most important decision you make is to be in a good mood. Never make a permanent decision based on a temporary emotion or feelings. Make emotions work for you instead of against you. I always remind myself that this moment is only temporary.

Experience the world personally and live impersonally—if you take all things personally you will react, not respond, all the time. Our need to be special lures us into the shadow by causing us to develop agendas that set us apart from others. It's critical to investigate what drives our need for attention so we are able to cultivate healthy responses to our urges.

For example, a healthy relationship with money takes you out of the shadows. Take things impersonally—your reaction to me is a reflection of you. Living life on a personal level is pure arrogance. Shadow doesn't have light, but the light has all colours in it.

Recognising we are both will help you to learn acceptance and stop being in reactive mode—on an emotional roller-coaster.

Recommended Authors: Andrew Harvey, Carolyne Myss, Debbie Ford, Robert Johnson

Journey through scarcity to abundance

I've hesitated to share this story. Honestly, it feels vulnerable, and part of me feels scared to put it out there. But this experience shaped who I am today, and I know that sometimes sharing our truth can create the deepest connections and help others feel less alone.

SHADOW vs LIGHT

Shadow	Light
Dark has million answers	Light has one answer
Always has agenda and lies	Light doesn't have agenda, doesn't lie
Manipulates and has pay offs	It's honest, pure, open
Loves controlling and putting conditions	Loves releasing way and trusts
Responding in stories, excuses, grey, trying to get away with everything	Responding yes/no
Always justifies	

For years after moving to Australia, I worked tirelessly—pushing, striving, and chasing after success. But no matter how hard I tried, it felt like I was stuck in the same cycle of exhaustion and disappointment. Everywhere I turned, I faced setbacks, discouragement, and people who mirrored the same energy I was feeling inside. I didn't always live this way, but at some point, I slipped into a state of desperation, feeling lost, and it held on tightly.

One of the defining moments of this period happened when I moved to Perth. I never really wanted to live there, but life took me there anyway. From the moment I stepped off the plane, something felt off. The dry heat, the endless wind, and the flat, unfriendly landscape all triggered discomfort I couldn't shake.

That discomfort turned to something deeper the first night I stayed in Perth. I ended up in Northbridge—one of the roughest areas, or simply "party" areas, of the city centre. I didn't know it at the time, but I felt the weight of the place almost instantly.

I remember sitting by the window, eating dinner with my partner, and staring out at the street below. What I saw honestly shocked me. There were people wandering around, aimless—a lot of junkies, drunks, homeless. I hadn't seen anything like that before. In Slovakia, where I grew up, those kinds of people and scenes were probably kept at home rather than in public. We may have fewer homeless because of the cold weather back home.

That night haunted me. It was just one experience, but it planted something dark in me that stayed for years. The energy of that night seemed to follow me as I tried to settle into the city.

Determined to build something new, I threw myself into the job hunt. I sent out more than 1,020 résumés, applying for anything that aligned with my skills and experience. But nothing came of it. No emails, no invitations for interviews—nothing.

With every rejection—or worse, the silence—I felt like I was shrinking, disappearing into the background. I started to believe that maybe I wasn't good enough. Maybe I would never succeed in Australia.

I kept going for over a year, but my health, both mentally and physically, began to suffer. I was exhausted, and despair slowly crept in. I convinced myself that maybe I didn't deserve the opportunities I was chasing.

To make matters worse, other parts of my life started to unravel. Very slow growth, almost none, in my business ventures, issues with business partners, unsuccessful IVF treatments, and a series of heartbreaks layered on top of the growing weight I was carrying. I began to lose faith—not just in the world around me, but in myself.

The lowest point came when I felt like I couldn't fight anymore. But instead of completely giving up, I decided to turn inward. I started to unravel the patterns that had quietly taken over my life—the limiting beliefs, the constant self-doubt, and the fear that I wasn't enough. I was looking for the happiest version of myself that I knew from my past. I've always been happy, playful, and courageous, but I couldn't even reach the glimpse of that feeling from my past.

One day, I made a bold decision to invest in myself and took a big leap in my business. I hired a marketing team to help launch a new venture, even though I barely had any money left. When they invoiced me for $2,200, I only had $750 in my account. It was a Friday I will never forget. I told myself, *I'll turn this around by Monday. I know I will.*

It felt like a leap off a cliff, but for the first time in a long while, I felt a shift. I finally trusted myself again. I held onto that belief with everything I had.

That Saturday, the breakthrough came. Out of nowhere, I received a long message from someone who needed my services—urgently. They didn't just hire me for a small project. They paid for six months of leadership coaching for their entire leadership team—more than enough to cover the invoice I had worried about and other important investments.

It felt like magic. But I knew deep down it wasn't magic at all. It was a reflection of the shift happening inside me, a manifestation of my state, energy, and vibration.

That moment changed everything.

From then on, things started to flow. Opportunities showed up in ways I couldn't have predicted. I met inspiring people who lifted me up, and slowly, I rebuilt the life I once dreamed of. Eventually, I relocated to another state and fulfilled a goal I had carried quietly for years. The abundance I longed for finally began to pour in.

Today, my life is full of joy and fulfilment. I create my path daily and help others along the way. But the biggest lesson wasn't in what I achieved—it was in realising that the **first things I needed to change were my mindset and emotions.**

I had to let go of scarcity and trust that I was worthy of more. And I had to believe it before I could see it.

If you're in that space where nothing seems to be working, I want you to know—your thoughts are powerful. When you shift your energy, the world shifts with you.

I know this because I've lived it.

Everything starts within.

I have another story. I met a very beautiful and capable woman. She became a client of mine. She was a successful, confident, and admirable woman who achieved so much success in the property industry in the past. Unfortunately, she trusted the wrong people and she went through bankruptcy. The wrong people and wrong business deals. It can happen to anyone. She lost business and a lot of money and she became very unhappy. Her now ex-husband wasn't working very hard and wasn't offering the security that she needed so badly at that time. She slowly went downhill. She doubted herself. She felt lost for so long. She tried a different style of business. She tried multi-level marketing as a mum, and she thought that would be a great solution. Nothing truly worked. She tried a few different business ideas, but always came back to a few similar problems. She felt that something was not right, almost like she couldn't find herself again. She felt like she had this wrong perception of herself as a successful businesswoman in her head, and now she truly believes it was only her imagination. She wasn't a social media person; she didn't want to be on social media taking selfies, making silly videos, and informing the world about her life so they could buy from her. It felt wrong for her, and I believe this imagination and utilisation of social media is wrong in general. So I felt for her. She felt inadequate and built up a very strong resistance inside of her which she kept in her day-to-day for a very long time.

She struggled to believe she could do anything. She started to feel old and silly. She didn't know what else to do. Every business idea died after a while. She wasn't becoming richer or better. She was far away from reaching her desired outcomes and that made her very unhappy.

One day, she started to grasp the idea of mind and emotions. We were working together on confidence and looking for new proof of how amazing she is when she knows what she wants.

She started to study what she loved. She started to do more of what she loved. By building abundance, trust, and self-esteem within, she started to understand herself and her needs. Of course, everything became so clear and she couldn't believe she didn't see it. She had a passion for a totally different business and area of life. She loved property and building. She was thriving in that area and she was doing very well. She trusted herself in this area because it was her passion. It was bringing her joy. She created abundance because she knew she found her way before she made extra dollars. She knew it was going to happen because she gained clarity and faith in herself.

She is now creating an amazing lifestyle for her and her kid. She is doing well and, most importantly, she is a happy single mum. She doesn't need to live in insecurity anymore. She lives in abundance, joy, and fulfillment. Everything she experienced, she turned around.

Why am I sharing these stories?

Because I want to show you how easy it can be and bring more proof to you so you can see you have it all in your hands.

What have I learnt from my clients?

That building wealth and lifestyle you want starts in your mind.

And I learnt how.

It all starts with breaking free from the inner limitation of fears and insecurities. Breaking free from not being able to dream and see a better future for yourself because it feels so far away. Learning how to believe in it and how to receive it. Learning that you can only reach the heights of your mind and inner world, so it's important to dream bigger and create a vision for your life.

Secondly, when you have your vision clarified, you can then start building your inner mood and feeling like you already have this perfect life.

No-one got wealthy or successful from a place of self-doubt or low self-esteem. It is the same with speakers. The only good speaker is the one who believes in what they share with the audience. If you build your vision and beliefs enough, they become contagious. People will want to support you and be around you because of your strong belief in the greater good. If you are a leader without vision and belief, no-one will want to follow you. It is not inspiring. Now, to clarify, making a certain amount of money is not a vision. I mean *meaningful* vision. I can share an example. I just met an amazing building company and the only reason I contacted them was because their vision is "We are doing good things with good people."

When I walked into the company reception and waited for my next meeting, I was amazed. I was taken care of by everyone who passed by. They shook my hand and they asked me if I was taken care of and if I needed anything while waiting. I couldn't believe how amazing it feels when you see vision in action.

If you are trying to become a great leader, you must first build your inner world. You need to understand who you are and if where you are is the right fit for your values and beliefs and your own vision. If all answers are "Yes, I am here at the right place and fully aligned", you can start creating your vision and values with your team. Help your team members to believe in something greater than themselves. That's your role as a leader. But if you don't fully trust your team vision, your team members, and yourself it's going to be a very bumpy road to success if that would be even the result.

Now, let's say you believe in yourself. You believe in your capabilities and your purpose.

You have a vision. You believe this vision is your true purpose now. Can you see how much energy is in this already and how much easier will be to communicate this vision to your team?

Imagine the opposite. You had to buy into some company vision you don't even believe. You are not sure if you are a great leader and if you have enough capabilities to lead people towards this vision. Can you see how hard it will be to even communicate to your team where you need to go? Does this feel a bit lost? How can the team members trust you if you are presenting the vision without emotional connection?

Can you see why this internal work is the most important? Would you be following a leader who doesn't even believe the vision is possible? Or would you follow the leader who has big dreams and vision and, although you may feel it's impossible, he believes in it so strongly that you have to trust him and want to join him?

Can you see and feel what is a true life force, life energy? It is actually created from beliefs. From within.

Leadership from within

I met Emily in a bustling city nestled between towering skyscrapers and busy streets with a crazy amount of offices and a hectic working lifestyle. Emily had always dreamed of becoming a leader, someone who could inspire and guide others towards greatness. But as she climbed the corporate ladder, she found herself feeling increasingly lost and disconnected from her true purpose. The corporate environment sickens a lot of poor souls.

One day, while reflecting on her journey, Emily realised that she had been chasing someone else's vision, someone else's dream. She had been trying to fit into a mould that didn't align with her values and beliefs. Deep down, she knew that she needed to start on a journey of self-discovery to uncover her true inner world.

With determination and courage, Emily set out on this journey, exploring her passions, strengths, beliefs, and core values. She dived deep into her soul, seeking clarity and alignment with her purpose. Along the way, she encountered challenges and obstacles, but with each hurdle she overcame, she grew stronger and more resilient.

As Emily connected with her inner world, she began to trust herself and her capabilities as a leader. She cultivated a vision that resonated deeply with her heart and soul, a vision that she believed in with every fibre of her being. This new-found sense of clarity and purpose infused her with boundless energy, potential, and enthusiasm.

With her inner world aligned, Emily stepped into her new role as a leader with confidence and conviction. She was prepared. She shared her vision with her new team, inspiring them to believe in something greater than themselves. Her authenticity and passion sparked a fire within each team member, creating a sense of purpose and drive.

As Emily led her team towards their shared vision, even through challenges and obstacles, she stayed true to a higher purpose. Emily believed so deeply in their mission that her strong faith and determination inspired her team to persevere through adversity. The team became much stronger because of her passion and the beliefs she shared. Passion and enthusiasm are contagious.

In the end, Emily and her team achieved remarkable success, not only in reaching their goals but also in forging great relationships and deep bonds of trust and respect. And as they celebrated their achievements together, Emily knew that the most important journey she had undertaken was the one within herself. For it was through this inner work that she had discovered the true source of life force and energy—the power of belief.

Imagine how many possibilities lie within you. By knowing and understanding that everything starts within you, can create whatever you want in your life. Strong faith, belief in a higher vision, and staying true to this vision will impact people you meet on the way, not just your direct team.

Self-effectiveness is the start

If we are talking about positive or effective leadership, there are some main elements we need to take care of and master. I tried to simplify concepts that have truly influenced me and my clients. The elements we teach in our leadership programs are very simple. Those three elements are:

- Efficacy
- Agency
- Self-esteem

Efficacy

This is an individual's confidence in their ability to demonstrate leadership behaviours like decision-making, delegating, motivating others and themselves, and pursuing their goals and organisational goals. It is believing in your leadership competence. It is believing you are able to manage yourself and others on the way towards one united vision.

Efficacy, in its essence, is rooted in our personal belief in our capacity to exhibit leadership qualities. It's about the confidence we hold in our ability to make decisions, delegate effectively, inspire others, and forge a path toward both personal and organisational objectives. It's a fundamental trust in our leadership prowess.

A multitude of elements shape our efficacy:

- **Confidence—self-belief.** We talked about this belief in the past chapters. We are focusing on gaining a true inner belief that you are capable of more than you can imagine.

- **Performance achievements.** Past successes and accomplishments serve as the bedrock of our efficacy. They are the tangible markers of our competence. It is great to build up your positive achievements, but don't forget that any small achievement counts. Don't wait until you achieve your biggest goal. Set up some smaller milestones so you can see the real small achievements that are important on a day-to-day basis.

- **Experiences.** Our journey, replete with experiences—both triumphs and setbacks—moulds our perception of our own capabilities. Each encounter leaves an imprint on our sense of efficacy. Build up confidence from your past experiences so you can clearly see you are more than able to overcome setbacks and challenges if you are in the right mind and mood.

- **Psychological state.** The state of our mind, be it one of confidence or doubt, significantly influences our efficacy. A positive mental outlook and a more optimistic mind bolsters belief in our leadership aptitude.

Now, how can we leverage these factors to fortify our efficacy?

Taking incremental steps. Building self-efficacy is akin to ascending a staircase one step at a time. It begins with small, consistent strides toward our objectives. What truly works is to understand what we want—what are the ideal results, for example, in all areas of our life, career, health, relationships, finance, or spiritual development. We need to understand how we can get there. Knowing your milestones and the steps towards these results will help you to build up small achievements on the way there.

Embracing opportunities and challenges. Each opportunity and challenge is a crucible for growth. By embracing them, you not only bolster your skill set but also augment your belief in your capacity to lead.

Exposure and role models. Modelling is a great tool to start with, especially at the beginning of your journey. Choose who your role models are. Choose more than one and focus on the attitudes or behaviours they have that you want to demonstrate too. If you don't have a direct boss, leader, or mentor who can help you, try to find your own outside of your circle. Being exposed to diverse scenarios and observing accomplished role models provides a valuable framework for developing your own efficacy.

Acknowledgement and personal growth. Recognising your achievements and dedicating yourself to ongoing personal and emotional development is vital. It reaffirms your progress and cultivates a continuous cycle of growth. I always say that when you stop learning, you start dying. Some people think that quote is nasty. I strongly believe it is true.

In essence, cultivating efficacy is a dynamic process set from your experiences, achievements, and the deliberate steps you take toward your goals. It is the foundation upon which impactful leadership is built.

Action Exercise: Group Exercise—Exercise To Develop Self-Efficacy

1. What is one challenge or opportunity for future growth that you can think of and you may be able to expose yourself to?
2. What is the one personal achievement you can acknowledge?
3. What is one wellness or emotional competence practice (habit) you can implement into your daily life?
4. Create a self-development plan.

5. Practise acknowledgement—write down ten achievements you can acknowledge every month. Over time, you will start seeing your progress optimistically and build a strong self-belief.

Agency

In my words, this is the skill of leadership or self-leadership. What is it? Why is it important?

It is the practice of understanding who you are, identifying your desired experience and outcomes and intentionally guiding yourself and others towards that.

Basically, it is the **determination of what we do, why we do it, and how we do it.**

To build agency and self-leadership, we need to build capabilities in three areas:

1. Optimistic mindset
2. Powerful mindful communication
3. Purposeful action

I will give you some cognitive and behavioural strategies to develop self-agency:

- **Self-awareness.** The ability to perceive yourself through inward inspection. It encompasses skills like self-control and self-regulation—what are our drivers, motivators, needs, and values?—and understanding your personal traits, strengths, weaknesses, talents, and interests. Improving awareness will bring more confidence into your life.
- **Identifying your goals and outcomes.** Understand how to align your goals or desired experiences with your values. This is important for being motivated to pursue your goals.
- **Thinking patterns.** Your ability to reason is inhibited when you feel stressed and are experiencing the so-called fight-or-flight response or amygdala hijack. When we are relaxed and in a positive state of emotions, we can think creatively and innovatively. We can utilise

more of the right brain, which is the creative brain and intuitive brain. This includes developing a growth mindset—the belief in our ability to develop and change things or ourselves. A growth mindset is a state where you are open to ideas and seek and create without using too much of the logical or data-driven left part of the brain. It also includes understanding that while we cannot control all of our experiences, we can control how we choose to react or respond to them. Practise mindfulness to help you to discover more understanding of your thinking. Pause and try to create a moment of stillness.

- **Planning**. Break bigger dreams into manageable milestones and then optimise each milestone into a goal. You can use the well-known SMART goals process, where S stands for *specific*—goals should be clear and well-defined, focusing on a specific outcome or result. This helps provide clarity and direction, ensuring everyone knows exactly what needs to be accomplished. M stands for *measurable*—goals should include criteria for measuring progress and success. This allows for tracking and evaluation, enabling individuals or teams to assess their performance and make adjustments as needed. A stands for *achievable*—goals should be realistic and attainable, considering the resources, skills, and time available. Setting achievable goals prevents frustration and boosts motivation by setting targets that are within reach. R stands for *relevant*—goals should be relevant and aligned with broader objectives or priorities. They should contribute to the overall mission or purpose, ensuring that efforts are focused on activities that matter. T stands for *time-bound*—goals should have a defined timeframe or deadline for completion. This creates a sense of urgency and helps prevent procrastination, motivating individuals or teams to take action and work efficiently towards their objectives. Basically, you create your goals with clarity and real detail. Identify contingency plans, document everything, establish accountability, and use positive rewards. Decide how often you are tracking. Sit down every week and evaluate what has happened and what hasn't and what can be improved.

- **Harnessing the ecosystem**. Proactively seek support for your goal behaviour in the social, organisational, community, political, and physical environment you live in. Nature versus nurture—the influence on our behaviour of our environment versus our genetics.

We can re-create who we are. I always remind people to please choose who they are, who they want to become, and what environment they want to be part of. We mostly learn our behaviour through our lives, circumstances, experiences, and the people around us. Some people think it is all mostly inherited, but we know now that there is a real power within us and the possibility to change ourselves and our genes.

Self-esteem

Great achievers and leaders have high self-esteem and positive self-image. They value themselves and feel worthy. The way you feel inside and the beliefs and ideas that you have about yourself are going to guide the way you perform on the outside and how you feel about others. Great achievers and leaders believe in themselves and have faith in others and their teams. They have self-confidence without being arrogant. They are confident because they feel as if they have credibility and something to contribute.

How can we recognise if we or others have high self-esteem? Here are some examples I noticed in successful people around me:

- They don't mind failure, because their ego can stand being wrong.
- They don't mind delegating, because they don't need to take glory all the time and they trust their team members. They can let go and they don't feel like they need to be in control all the time.
- They are aware of what they offer to their team and organisation.
- They don't micromanage, because they understand they need to give responsibility and accountability to their team.
- They speak out against wrongdoing, because they aren't scared of losing their jobs or having hard conversations.
- They raise concerns in a very kind way, but they speak up and don't hold a grudge or bottle up anger.
- They are trusting and they are trustworthy.
- They understand the importance of reputation and "walking the talk".

How to build self-esteem:

1. Remember times when you succeeded and recall the moment of happiness, freedom, or success. See the image or visual expression of that moment.

2. Connect to your old image of a successful day and go back to the feeling when you were happier or maybe proud of yourself or just felt grateful, free, satisfied, and loving. Recall any image that reminds you of a great feeling of love or connection. The important thing here is to feel it again. When you recall such a moment, you should feel it in your body.

3. Keep this feeling in your body and sit with it. Let it become a part of your day-to-day practice so your body gets addicted to this positive feeling.

Another great way to build your self-esteem is to become more open and find peers you can speak to about issues you are facing and brainstorm solutions with others. You are not alone. Asking questions is the best way to succeed. Ask your team members or ask someone to mentor you if you feel like that is what you need. Find your coach or guide to progress.

Learn lessons when you fail and write down what you can do better next time. The most important thing in life is stepping out of your comfort zone. Start to get comfortable with discomfort.

Sometimes we are blind to our own limits. I was a great example of that a decade ago. I was struggling at a new place, starting a new business and pretending I had it all together. One day, I attended a business event from a different perspective and a different mind. Instead of judging myself and others, I was there listening and thinking about who could become my mentor. For the first time in my life, I got excited about asking for help. I saw it as a major mindset shift because before, I was competing with others. This was a great stepping stone for me to see how many people actually want to help. Everyone I asked for a meeting met me that month. Everyone was very open and helpful and moved me in the right direction. This was a real deal for me to ask strangers for help. But I realised I didn't have the network and I was new in this place, so why not ask the best people in their field where to go next? This is important, especially when you want to change your environment. If you don't have a lot of opportunities where you are right now, connect with new groups, new communities, and new people and see how amazing people are when you ask for help.

Try it.

Ask Yourself

Action Exercise: Self-Esteem Check:

When was the last time you stepped out of your comfort zone?

Action Exercise to Develop Self-Agency

1. What is the goal or outcome you want this year?
2. What motivates you and what drives you? Do your own values discovery exercise from this book. It helps you to understand what motivates you.
3. What is the circle you are in right now, and does that serve you, or do you need to look for a new circle to learn from? Do you need a mentor in the area you want to improve? Look for the best.

Now let's do a little more self-coaching.

Self-coaching—emotions

Coaching questions using emotions

Let's have a look at how we can use a self-coaching model with emotions or how you can coach yourself or your team members. I truly enjoy self-coaching, journalling, going deeper into what I am feeling, and deepening my understanding. These are just examples of questions I use for self-coaching when I am trying to release tension and when I am trying to learn from emotions and feelings I feel.

Imagine an event that occurred or happened around you, to your teammate, or to you. Use the following questions to identify resistance or emotions connected to this event and how this influenced you or what you can learn.

COACHING QUESTIONS USING EMOTIONS:

- How does that situation make you feel?
- What happened just before you felt that emotion?
- Can you identify the underlying cause that triggered that emotion?
- Is the emotion you're experiencing helping you in this situation?
- What thoughts or beliefs are contributing to this emotion?
- What do you see or perceive that reinforces this emotion?
- Where is your attention primarily directed when you feel this way?
- Would you like to change this emotional response?
- How would you prefer to feel instead?
- How are your current emotions influencing your behaviour?
- In what ways are you avoiding certain behaviours due to these feelings?
- How would you like to behave differently in this situation?
- How do you notice your emotions affecting your actions and decisions?
- What signs will indicate that you consciously chose this feeling in the future?
- How can you create a moment of pause to shift your emotional direction?
- What signals will show you that you are successfully changing your emotions?
- What advantages would come from adopting a more resourceful emotion?
- How would others benefit from witnessing this shift in your emotions?
- What new opportunities or abilities would this emotional shift provide you with?

- What habits or actions will you no longer engage in with this new emotional response?

Life with Meaning quiz

I had a massive breakthrough and insights about trying to "fit in", especially during the time when I moved to Perth, WA. When I realised that I could be myself and I could stand out, my identity shifted and I tapped into new energy and frequencies. This profound experience was so impactful that I couldn't stop thinking or talking about it.

Why is that?

Because I realised I'm not alone. Almost 95% of my clients experience the same thing—the same pressure of trying to be someone else or fit in.

We often live on autopilot without knowing we have set ourselves up to keep living by the expectations of others. Sometimes, it can be still by the expectations of our parents even though we are in our forties. It can be that we created an image of how we should be as a good parent, friend, or partner and we keep living in that image or with the criteria of expectations from ourselves but not others. We make up these expectations without knowing. We think our kids want us more at home. We think our kids want to play with us or our partner wants us to keep cooking their dinner. But who said that? Usually us. We create this made-up identity and we live by that for so long that we become someone else. Later in life, we realise we are not living authentically.

When this happens, when you realise your life is based on someone else's expectations, it creates a big shift, because you are quite settled on the trajectory of your life. Most people, at this stage, are not going through massive changes, anyway; they're mostly trying to avoid the change. This part of your life is when you are living day-to-day in a very routine way. It is almost like it all happens without consciously thinking about it. Somehow, you live like this year after year, making decisions in comfort, with goals that are not too big or ambitious—just normal life. A little sad, sometimes full of bad luck, and sometimes feeling unfulfilled and empty. Sometimes too angry or frustrated for no reason. Sometimes or most of the time self-doubting without realising that you decide to live this life. Your choice is based on someone else's choice that was projected on you in the past. One example is my dad. I love him dearly, but when I was eighteen, I truly wanted to study psychology at university. I felt in my bones that it was all I wanted. It was a different time, a different generation. I had to listen to my dad's advice to take economics at university. So I studied economics. I wanted to quit so many times. I didn't enjoy it—not because it was difficult, but because I had no passion for it. I finished school, got my master's, and for a very long time, I lived in business and numbers and just did things the way I learnt in economics. I felt like he took away my dream of studying and practising psychology. He said that there was no-one who would pay me for psychological advice. It was true at that time. No-one was hiring psychologists or coaches and paid for it. At least not then. There were no private psychologists; at least, it wasn't that common. But it changed. It changed a few years after I finished economics, so I would have been fine. I didn't fight for my authenticity and my dreams hard enough. And here we go. I am back in psychology and coaching more than a decade later. It took me so long to recognise that I was living my dad's expectations, not my life. It is such a small thing, and we forget who we are—we forget about our dreams and desires. We forget what our passion is.

If you are living someone else's life and not living a life for you and who you are, it's time to look at that. It's time to discover your own authenticity and uniqueness.

If you stay on the trajectory of living the way so you fit in and satisfy other's expectations, you will be very unhappy later in life and you will feel lost and empty. Don't live on autopilot, and stop living a mostly unconscious life. Start thinking about who you are inside. What is a real expression of yourself? What you didn't express in the past few years? What dreams did you give up on?

Living your life in a state of trying to fit in leads to stress, exhaustion, and burnout.

Life with Meaning Quiz

I created these ten questions to raise awareness about where you are operating from and where your decision-making comes from—what state you are in. Are you operating too often or almost all the time from the amygdala (fight-or-flight mode) and leading yourself to burnout, exhaustion, and life without meaning?

Answer these questions YES or NO.

QUESTIONS:

1. Do you often find yourself feeling physically and emotionally drained, almost to the point of burnout?
2. Have you noticed that you struggle to truly enjoy your free time without work-related thoughts or tasks creeping in?
3. Would you describe yourself as a workaholic, where work seems to dominate a significant portion of your life?
4. Do you feel like the joy and satisfaction you used to derive from your career or business has diminished over time?
5. Have you experienced a notable decline in your motivation and inspiration levels in recent times?
6. Are you currently at a crossroads, where you have achieved a certain level of success but find yourself questioning the purpose and direction of your endeavours?
7. Have you noticed a shift in your ability to identify what truly brings you happiness and fulfilment?
8. Do you often feel overwhelmed and find yourself constantly racing against the clock, struggling to find enough time in a day?
9. Have you come to realise that you've been wearing a metaphorical mask for much of your life, potentially leading to a sense of disconnection from your authentic self?
10. Do you feel like you've lost touch with your inner self, resulting in a feeling of disconnect or even a sense of "floating" through life?

What are your results?

If you answer YES on 1–3 questions, you are in a stress zone (operating up to 60% of the time from the amygdala) and you need to bring awareness to the thinking and emotional patterns that drive your life. It would be great to take care of your self-awareness at this point before it's too late and before your life becomes automated.

If you answered 4–6 YES, it indicates you are operating more than 60% of your time from the amygdala (living in stress mode—fight-or-flight is on almost all the time). You should take a step back and start looking at your life, what is missing, what you are expressing, and what you are suppressing, and bring awareness to those feelings and patterns that need to be shifted.

If you answered YES to seven or more, you are in true danger of being burnt out right now. You are operating 80% of the time in stress mode, from the amygdala, making decisions and choices from this space. You are creating a business or career in this state, and it is very dangerous and, most of the time, not authentic. You need to take an urgent step forward and connect to yourself, because every day, you are further from your true self and your purpose.

If you are already operating from the amygdala, and you are not living your authentic life, it's time to look at this closely. I would suggest finding yourself a good guide, coach, or mentor. If you are not prepared to deal with it yet, you can find a lot of resources and free tools on our website.

Even reading this book will help you to understand yourself better and take you to a higher awareness so you can start building your true life with meaning.

Regain your power and authenticity

Why even think about authenticity?

The majority of people live and guide their lives from the part of their brain called the amygdala (the fight-or-flight centre). From this centre, they are often worried about money, their career, future, kids, relationships, or their health and wealth and live in an anxious state, sometimes resulting in numbness. When they operate in this mode, they feel like they are living in some kind of limbo waiting for something to happen, or they find themselves stuck.

They are not sure where to go next, or they wonder where they have gone, as they don't recognise themselves. So, before they even reflect on themselves, they learn one of the most common behavioural patterns—busyness, or being busy with low-value activities. They are doing something all the time and when they stop, the feeling of guilt and shame starts sneaking in and it becomes an ongoing and never-ending cycle until it is too late or until burnout. People feel like there is only progress and life in movement and ongoing activity, but they never realise there is more learning and progress in stillness than they ever imagined. There is a space and state where you can tap into your authenticity.

In stillness, you see, you learn, you understand, and you gain clarity like never before.

There is another very common constant fear of hurting other people's feelings, so they lie. They are packaging the truth in nice words and never give honest feedback because they want others to like them and not be judged or even hated. This is living in resistance. This is being "nice", not being kind. This is truly a very inauthentic way to live, because all you are doing is lying to yourself and not living your truth.

I can give you an example from this morning. Without awareness, I would end up doing something that is against my values and my beliefs, but I'm trying to make most of my decisions with full consciousness and authenticity.

My fellow coach asked me to give him a video testimonial for the course I attended two years ago. We were taught to support each other and help each other with recommendations and endorsements, but when I tried to recall the four-week program, I only got a lot of bad feelings, anger, frustration, and disappointment. I was searching for why I felt that way and what actually created this state, so I was not able to create an honest video endorsement.

I realised that one of the coaches, who was supposed to be the head coach of the program and who sold me the program in the first place, didn't show up as a facilitator at all. It wasn't okay with me, because I was buying him and his skills and experience as a facilitator. Also, there was another thing—he didn't communicate this to us clearly. We never knew if he was going to show up to the session and, secretly, we were hoping he would. I was surprised there was no transparency and no communication about this and that no-one raised the issue. I was very frustrated, but I kept that to myself for so long.

I believe that, if I knew how to be authentic at the time, I wouldn't be carrying this feeling with me now. Also, if I had been brave enough, I would have raised the issue openly and calmly at the time, and we all would have ended up with solutions and ideas for how to move forward in the program. Well, that was my learning opportunity, and I grew so much from that. I know now that raising concerns, giving and receiving feedback humbly and openly, and expressing expectations and concerns before it is too late is healthier and also can serve others.

Being transparent and authentic are truly the most important characteristics of a high-quality life and leadership. Now, two years later, I had to tell them how I feel and why I couldn't offer the endorsement—which felt difficult, because I would have loved to give them good feedback. I couldn't do it, though, because it wouldn't have been honest. This wasn't entirely their fault—it was mine as well, because I didn't speak up or point out the problem when it first arose, not only for me but for others too.

I held onto that feeling, even though I know feelings don't belong to us. They are only experiences of life. So, don't prolong your suffering. Start looking for a real expression of yourself.

Operating and creating life or business from a state of being "nice" but not authentic or kind is dangerous. It risks disconnecting you from your inner self, leading to a loss of authenticity and true joy. It's like living in a lie and the pressure of not expressing the truth in a clear and kind way. This often results in burnout, anxiety, demotivation, exhaustion, and disappointment. Leading your career or business from this place of inauthenticity creates distance between you and your colleagues, friends, or family. How can you lead yourself and positively impact those around you if you're disconnected from your truth? It's not possible, and it certainly isn't sustainable. Also, people can't get to know you and can't connect with you because you are not yourself.

Creating and living life from the amygdala (fight-or-flight mode) brings countless issues. I experienced exhaustion and burnout by trying to fit in—working fourteen-hour days, weekends, and taking almost no breaks because I was pressured by a feeling of not being enough, not belonging, and feeling like there was not enough for nearly seven years. My focus was on increasing revenue and business growth. I achieved some results, but the energy exchange wasn't equal. I wasn't truly gaining the joy or fulfillment I expected.

I didn't have time to enjoy the progress or the journey itself. Later, I realised I didn't want to continue like that—without fun, joy, or time for family, friends, and travel. It became clear that even if I made more money, nothing really changed. I just felt more exhausted and disconnected.

That's why I began this journey of understanding human brains, emotions, and spirituality—to learn how we can feel happiness and joy while being present in our day-to-day activities, creating wealth in alignment with who we are and what we truly want.

I started to research not only myself but also my clients who felt the same, especially those working hard and going through burnout or exhaustion.

I realised a lot of successful people felt the same and were also confused. They felt like they lost track of their true selves, what they believe in, and why they do what they do. The true purpose was blurry and there was no meaning. Some of my clients thought they were working that hard to help their family, their parents, or others around them. Slowly, they realised that it was only their belief, subconscious program, and subconscious perception that they had to do it for others because it was expected, without realising that people would rather experience their company no matter how much money they have. Kids and partners would appreciate them more if they were happy and had fun with their own kids even without success and money.

They realised they didn't need to do it and they actually only *thought* others expected them to work hard and create wealth and success. That wasn't true. And still, they found themselves running on autopilot with limiting beliefs as a driver and guide of their behaviour. One of my clients said, "I actually realised my family never thought I should do it. It was my inner voice coming from insecurities and fear or probably regrets."

They started to change with increased self-awareness. Started to build a deep connection with themself and disconnect from the amygdala. They were able to connect to true inner love, and joy came into their life. They started to attract and magnetise what they wanted in their life and started working fewer hours, more effectively, with more love and passion and created better results than ever before. When I heard my clients talking about changes such as taking time off, going for holidays, playing on the beach with kids or taking them camping, buying a new house in the beautiful countryside instead of the city without even thinking about it, or starting to leverage and delegate in their business so they have time for their health, my heart was singing because I knew they started living their life more authentically. They are listening to their own needs and caring more. Without self-care, you are blindly pretending that you care for others, but subconsciously, you are hurting them and yourself. When you start to care for yourself and show yourself respect and love, you realise what others around you truly need. You will start to see what you didn't see before.

You will gain clarity and place yourself in a very great observer seat of reality.

Emotional Fitness

In personal and professional development, understanding and mastering emotional fitness sets itself apart from traditional cognitive and technical training. To me, it is the most important piece of training and skills to gain to build up a healthy life and influential leadership. It requires a distinctive approach—one that explores the depths of our emotions and how to deal with emotions and human connections.

It's great to learn the structure of the business, the impact of each department, strategic thinking, setting up vision, mission, goals, measuring, and delegating. But let me explain. For example, to start delegating from a technical point of view, our program will give you tools with a few questions and directions on what to delegate from the perspective of high-value activities. You assess yourself and you take action. But we realised there was a missing point—the emotional shift before every behavioural change; in our case, before delegating. A lot of people took the piece of paper with new activities and delegated activities and tried to follow the process. But in most cases, the second day or week later, managers found themselves doing the jobs again, or they started to feel agitated, nervous, or stressed, and they micromanaged or controlled people who were doing the delegated tasks. It created more anxiety and worries than before.

Why is that?

Because they didn't shift on the emotional level. They didn't fully trust their staff, or they didn't believe in their capabilities and the level of ownership. They internally didn't let go, because if they stopped doing what they were comfortable with and good at, they would feel less worthy and important. As you can see, our ego plays a big role in emotional fitness. There is so much emotional baggage in the leadership world. And it's normal, because we didn't learn to do it the new way. We still are getting promotions based on our technical skills, so it's hard to let go of our technical mastery. That is understandable.

What is the solution then?

The CEB method is the key to cultivating highly emotionally fit leaders and teams. We're shifting away from behaviour-centric leadership, recognising its inefficacy and steering towards leadership rooted in understanding, responding appropriately, and acting for the greater good. It is about acceptance first. Now, it's important to understand the word *acceptance*. A lot of people are surprised when I mention acceptance. They ask me, "Do you mean to watch and do nothing?"

Well, not exactly.

It does not mean to accept all I see and do nothing. It means to accept the emotions and reality for what they are and respond adequately without reaction or emotional outburst, without making it all about yourself, and without listening to your ego. It means to accept that there is good and bad, there is shadow and light in everything—in other people and within you. It's okay. The major thing is to learn to stop overreacting and make it about yourself—to let shadow put you into a victim state.

My aim is to humanise leadership, embracing simplicity despite the inherent complexity of human beings, and navigating the emotional and thinking world more deliberately. Understanding yourself and your emotions first before you start leading people from an inner place is the most important step into great leadership.

It's not very healthy to lead people from a state of worry, mistrust, or doubt. In this state, it is impossible to build trust. If you are experiencing a feeling of not trusting your people and being scared of relying on them, it's coming from within. It is like a cycle. Someone needs to break that cycle and decide to trust. The question is, is that you?

Startling statistics reveal that American businesses are haemorrhaging billions annually due to their oversight of the pivotal role emotional intelligence plays in their operations. Australia's figures are likely not far behind.

However, some conscious business leaders grasp this concept. They comprehend that genuine success extends beyond intellect or skills; it hinges on personal qualities such as grit, confidence, awareness, self-discipline, and the ability to connect with others. Think of those "super salespeople" who intuitively understand customer desires and build trust or the customer service experts who can transform irritated clients into reasonable individuals through conversation.

Conversely, there are executives who excel in everything but struggle with human interaction, hindering their careers. There are managers with technical brilliance but who crumble under stress, leaving their potential untapped because they never build up interpersonal skills and emotional fitness.

The good news is that emotional learning and behavioural change can be nurtured at any life stage. It's entirely plausible to transform individuals into workplace emotional intelligence experts.

I started to work with one engineer who was the COO of a manufacturing company in the tech and automation area. He was living and operating from his left brain the majority of the time—the intellectual, analytical part of the brain. He was very disconnected from his own emotional body. His posture and body language were saying, *I am better than you and I know it.* It was overconfidence coming from his ego. He was scared of failing and making mistakes. He was always right. He was always talking at the meetings and arguing his truth. He wasn't listening to others.

I was sitting in their big boardroom, hoping I was there to work with the CEO, but he explained that I was going to start with the COO first. When I saw his look, and probably mine as well, it said a lot. I wasn't very impressed because it felt almost impossible to transform this person into someone emotionally fit who actively listens and connects with others. At the start, there was a lot of pushback and a bit of defensiveness.

Fast-forward seven months later, and the COO became a new person. He transformed into a kind, open, and mindful person who had amazing experiences of deep connections with people around him. When he was telling me about his experience, he said he'd had to leave conversations because he was so connected that he felt what the other person was feeling. He developed a deep sense of empathy, and he started meditation and deep inner work. I was very excited to see that he was performing better. He had integrated a new culture into his company, with new sets of values and open conversations with his team. New systems and processes came into place and new development and learning structures, together with high-level values-aligned hiring and induction processes. All because he started to listen and see what his people needed and how he could best drive their behaviours. He moved from control to influence. He moved from inner worries, fear, and self-doubt to confidence and peace.

Now, look at this from a big-picture perspective. If engineers, financial planners, or accountants—highly data-driven and analytical people—can transform into highly conscious people, anyone can. Those highly analytical people moved into the right brain more often, and this led to higher performance and massive shifts in company success and profitability.

As you see, sustainable growth and positive results are the results of the ability to change from within.

However, many leadership programs miss the mark by failing to acknowledge the profound distinction between regular learning and the unique realm of emotional understanding and focus on transformation within. It's like comparing apples and oranges—entirely distinct, yet all equally crucial.

Emotions always cause bodily reactions and affect our bodies inwardly. For example, anger can cause grinding teeth, clenched fists, furrowed brows, and tightness of the face without being conscious of any of these.

We know that those emotions cause things we can see physically. Imagine what they cause inside your body and organs that we can't see.

Changing your emotions can heal your body, and you can feel vital and energised, or you can make your body ill.

Let's deep dive into the world of emotional learning and accord it the recognition it merits. Let's leverage the power of human emotions, understanding, and connection to unlock the full potential of ourselves and individuals in the workplace. After all, it's the heart and soul of success that propels the most remarkable achievements.

In Goleman's extraordinary framework of social awareness, we encounter a trio of captivating competencies: empathy, service orientation, and organisational awareness. At its heart, empathy is the profound art of embracing someone else's world, stepping into their shoes, and truly seeing the world through their eyes. It's about asking ourselves, "How would I feel if I were in their shoes?" It's a realm of genuine care and connection.

Those who embody this inspiring competence possess an unwavering attentiveness. They possess a unique gift of attuning themselves to the vast range of emotional signals that surround them. They are not only great listeners but are also masters at deciphering the unspoken emotions that dwell within individuals and groups.

These empathetic souls navigate life with a heightened sensitivity to others' perspectives and mindfulness. They hold the remarkable ability to grasp the depths of someone's needs and emotions, like an artist painting a vivid portrait of human understanding.

Empathy is an indispensable thread weaving its way through every facet of existence. It shines its light on every profession and role from parenthood and marriage to sales, education, medicine, and people management. It's the ethereal force that breathes life into our relationships and human interactions.

When empathy is absent, we stumble upon the shadows of indifference and uncaringness. A lack of genuine listening ruins communication, trust, and the foundation of harmonious working relationships. Yet, when empathy takes centre stage, it's as if a magical symphony unfolds, orchestrating deep connections, boundless trust, and effortless collaboration.

As coaches, we embark on a sacred journey with our clients. A journey where we encourage them to unlock the profound treasure trove of listening and empathy. It's a starting point that transforms relationships and human interactions. As we instil the importance of listening within our clients, we ignite a flame that can illuminate their lives and the lives of those around them.

In these empathetic relationships and connections, hearts open and souls unite. It's the transformative power that has the potential to reshape the world one person at a time. Let us embrace empathy with all our being and, through our leadership style and coaching, help others discover the magic that unfolds when we truly deeply listen and connect with others on a profound emotional level.

To truly embrace empathy, we must start a journey of quieting our minds and diving deeper into the unspoken needs of others. It's a profound art of listening not only to the words spoken but also to the whispers of someone's soul. Every moment, we must ask ourselves, "What does this person truly need right now?"

Is it care that they seek? A compassionate embrace that soothes their spirit? Or is it respect, the validation that they are seen and valued for who they are? Perhaps they yearn for recognition, a nod of acknowledgment that their efforts are noticed and appreciated. Or it could be the thirst for knowledge, the need to be informed and included in the happenings around them. Maybe they crave a challenge, an opportunity to grow and flourish beyond their boundaries.

It is in this introspective moment that we discover the essence of empathy. Our communication becomes a channel through which we reach out, assuring the other person that we truly understand or are sincerely trying to fathom what they might be feeling.

Yes let us beware of the allure of "psychologising," as Goleman phrases it. It is not empathising; it's imposing our own judgments and diagnoses on someone's emotions, trivialising their genuine feelings. Rushing to explain their feelings away with psychological causes of childhood roots disregards the profound significance of their emotions.

We must resist the temptation to venture into this realm and encourage our clients to do the same if they wish to cultivate empathy. It is vital not to invalidate the emotions of those we communicate with. Instead, let us embrace the gift of empathy, the art of truly listening and understanding the hearts of others without imposing our assumptions.

Through empathy, we create a world where souls connect, hearts are understood, and genuine and trustworthy bonds are formed. It is in this tender exchange of understanding that we find the seeds of compassion and the beauty of human connection. Let us tread this path of empathy with compassion and grace, fostering a world where empathy rises and souls are seen and heard.

If you wish to build more empathy, a great start is to listen to yourself. Understand what your feelings and emotions are telling you. What do your body and soul truly need? Can you answer the question?

It all starts with you. Ask yourself in a quiet moment when you are not distracted. Focus on your breath and emotions and the sensations in your body. "What do I truly need right now?"

You can start learning to listen by listening to your body and subconscious needs.

Chapter 6

Our Limitless Mind

Thoughts-emotions-body connection in leadership

Let me share with you a powerful and transformative experience I had with one of my clients here in Australia. Let's call him Jeff. Jeff is a highly successful individual who recently stepped into the role of CEO at a large building and manufacturing company.

As leaders, stepping into positions of influence within teams and organisations carries immense responsibility. Our ultimate goal must be to cultivate environments rooted in psychological safety, mental agility, and organisational health. This isn't just about boosting performance—it's about creating spaces where people feel secure enough to grow, innovate, and thrive without falling into the trap of victimhood.

However, there is a delicate balance. While focusing on mental health and fostering safety is crucial, we must ensure that psychological safety doesn't unintentionally become a shield for complacency or an excuse to avoid growth. The line between nurturing resilience and enabling victim mentality can be razor-thin. The challenge lies in protecting the wellbeing of employees without compromising the company's mission or enabling disempowering patterns.

So how do we master the art of leading others—and ourselves?

The truth is, leadership is not just about strategy, numbers, or performance metrics. At its core, leadership is about understanding human beings—truly seeing them, hearing them, and making them feel valued and understood.

People don't follow titles; they follow those who create space for their potential to be realised.

As facilitators of growth, we hold the incredible power to shape cultures that unlock greatness—where vulnerability and strength coexist, and where openness becomes the breeding ground for transformation. But to build these cultures, we must be willing to dive deep into the mechanics of the human mind, emotional fitness, and the behaviours that shape our realities. This is the foundation of conscious leadership.

Here's the thing—most leaders aren't psychologists. Nor do they need to be. Yet the most transformative leaders recognise that technical skills and expertise can only take them so far. Leadership isn't just about excelling in a job; it's about excelling in the art of connection and influence.

For far too long, leadership has been seen as a measure of competence and achievement. But the new era of leadership demands more—it demands heart, empathy, and the courage to explore the uncharted territories of human potential.

Jeff's story is a testament to this. As he stepped into his new role, he realised that fostering productivity alone wasn't enough. His true power as a leader lay in his ability to build trust, foster safety, and inspire those around him to believe in possibilities they couldn't yet see for themselves.

The moment Jeff embraced this, his influence grew. His company began to shift, not because of stricter policies or aggressive strategies, but because the collective energy transformed. And when the energy of a team shifts, the results follow.

True leadership begins when we recognise that mastering others starts with mastering ourselves.

I believe this has all changed over the past few years. We are pushed to learn about ourselves and others because our human needs have changed. They changed because we went through a lot of various crises over the past few years, which have made us look within and see the worst part of ourselves. Our core needs are less about wealth and more about being heard and understood. We want to speak up more and we want to live the life we deserve. So, leaders or business owners have a pretty hard job right now. In the past few chapters, you were able to grasp some growth tools and now, I will give you some more simple tools to use, especially as a leader, parent, or partner.

A key focus in our work is around mental agility and the art of reframing challenges. Coaching and mentoring are all about that, too. How can we best help people? To reframe so they can access new ways of thinking. Mental agility equips us with the ability to reframe obstacles into opportunities, even amidst stressful situations. And one of the most valuable tools to enhance mental agility is the practice of **reframing.**

Mental agility and how our brain works

Through reframing, we harness the power of our brain's flexibility, known as neuroplasticity, allowing it to adapt and form new neural connections. This neurological adaptability enables us to embrace change and develop innovative solutions.

In this journey, self-coaching models and the art of questioning and listening play a pivotal role. Every question we ask ourselves is a stepping stone towards creating new perspectives, enhancing neuroplasticity, and expanding our cognitive horizons.

The heart and soul of this chapter are focused on cultivating mental agility and fostering psychological safety. The key indicators of high mental agility include elevated self-awareness, social awareness, recognition of our strengths and blind spots, improved emotional regulation, and the ability to understand and overcome our fears and biases.

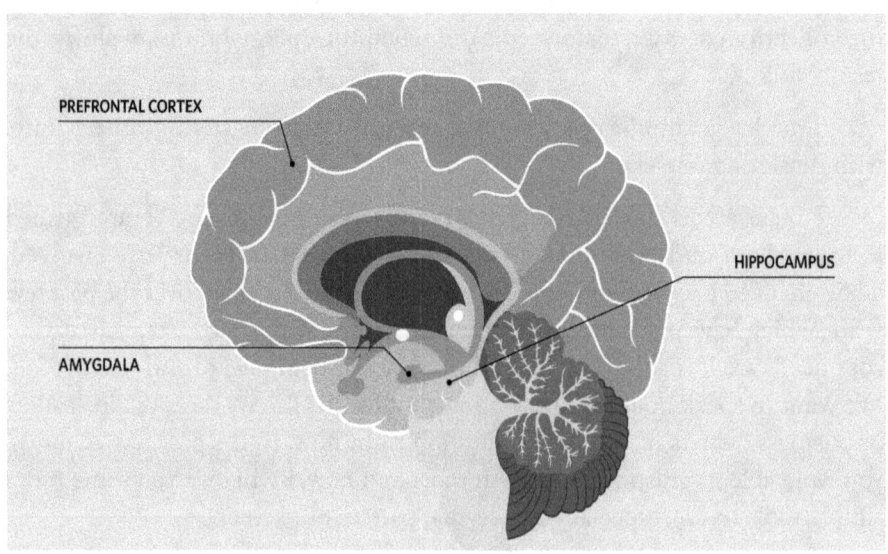

As we dive into the core of this journey, we equip ourselves and our teams with the resilience to face unforeseen challenges, the ability to respond with clarity rather than reacting impulsively thanks to lower amygdala reactions, and the fuel to drive innovation. Our journey towards excellence in listening and empathy further strengthens our leadership capabilities, allowing us to navigate through the complexities of life and leadership with confidence and competence.

Ultimately, this holistic training and development are geared towards empowering leaders to become an inspiration, instilling a sense of calm instead of chaos and nurturing a culture of growth and trust. By embracing the power of mental agility and psychological safety, we start on a transformative journey, lighting up the potential of every individual and paving the way for unparalleled achievements and success. As leaders, we become inspirations and drivers of change, paving the path for a brighter and more impactful future.

Every single thought that crosses our minds sets off a magnificent biochemical reaction in the brain. It's a dance of chemistry, where the brain creates specific chemical messengers that transmit signals to the body. These messengers are like couriers, rushing with vital information from the brain, influencing every cell in the body to respond in alignment with those thoughts. It's a breathtakingly rapid process, happening in less than milliseconds.

These chemical messengers come in three forms—neurotransmitters, neuropeptides, and hormones—each playing a vital role in brain activity and bodily functioning. Neurotransmitters are the messengers responsible for communicating between nerve cells, facilitating the seamless exchange of information throughout the brain and nervous system. Some neurotransmitters excite the brain while others calm it down or even regulate our sleep-wake cycles.

The second type of messenger, neuropeptides, takes centre stage. They form the majority of these chemical couriers, many of which are produced in the brain's intricate structure called the hypothalamus. These incredible chemicals also find their way to our immune system, proving just how interconnected our mind and body truly are. As neuropeptides travel through the bloodstream, they attach themselves to various cells, activating the third type of messenger: hormones. These hormones further influence our feelings, colouring our emotional landscape.

To put it simply, neurotransmitters mainly transmit messages from the brain and mind, neuropeptides serve as the bridge between our thoughts and bodily responses, and hormones primarily govern our feelings within the body. Now, you can clearly see that the CEB method is based on all bodily functions. Thoughts influence body response and state. Our state of mind creates emotions, and those produce hormones and are connected with chemicals in our body.

Imagine this: you contemplate confronting a colleague about a team issue they caused. The moment this thought arises, neurotransmitters begin their magic, firing up specific brain circuits that create a particular state of mind. As this thought journey continues, neuropeptides leap into action, relaying the chemical signals to your body, and suddenly, you start to feel a bit stirred up. These neuropeptides eventually find their way to your adrenal glands, urging them to release adrenaline and cortisol, causing you to feel increasingly fired up and ready for action. Your body is now chemically prepared for battle. This happens many times during the day, especially at this stage, when we are living in the amygdala.

This beautiful connection between our thoughts and emotions operates in a fascinating loop. As different thoughts emerge, the brain's circuits light up in corresponding patterns, producing levels of mind that match those thoughts perfectly.

Then, as if on cue, the brain generates specific chemicals that mirror those thoughts, so you can experience precisely the emotions you were thinking about. Thus, when you think of uplifting, loving, or joyous thoughts, your brain concocts chemicals that make you feel exactly that—uplifted, loving, and joyful. Conversely, if negative, fearful, or impatient thoughts take centre stage, the brain's chemical symphony quickly shifts, making you feel negative, anxious, or impatient in mere seconds.

This dance between mind and body, governed by intricate chemical interactions, underscores the profound interconnection between our thoughts and emotions. By understanding this intimate relationship, we gain profound insight into the power we hold to shape our feelings and, ultimately, our reality.

As we journey through life, something fascinating happens—our thoughts and feelings intertwine in a play, creating a profound connection between the mind and the body. This beautiful connection arises from the brain's constant communication with our body. It's a feedback loop of thoughts and emotions where the way we think influences how we feel and how we feel, in turn, influences how we think.

You see, thoughts primarily reside in the realm of the mind and the brain, while feelings are deeply rooted in the body. When our thoughts align with specific emotional states, the mind and body unite in harmony, giving birth to what we call a "state of being". This state of being becomes a vital part of our self-identity, defining who we are at the present moment. We declare our identity through phrases like "I am angry," "I am suffering," "I am inspired," "I am negative," or "I am insecure."

As the years go by, this union of thoughts and feelings solidifies, creating a memorised state of being. Our emotional body remembers those. Our thoughts and feelings become inseparable, and we embody these states with absolute certainty. We become so accustomed to these patterns that they become subconsciously programmed within us, shaping our behaviours, attitudes, beliefs, emotional reactions, habits, and perceptions.

By the time we reach our mid-thirties, our identity and personality are almost entirely formed. We carry within us a set of programmed behaviours, responses, and reactions that run us like well-oiled machines. We find ourselves thinking the same thoughts, feeling the same emotions, and reacting in identical ways. We attract the same drama, the same problems, and the same people or partners. We become like robots, operating mostly on our subconscious program.

But the key to change lies in thinking beyond how we feel and then shifting the way we feel consciously. By consciously rewiring our thoughts and embracing new perspectives, we can break free from the limitations of our subconscious programming. We can unlock the power to change our state of being and create a new reality for ourselves. It all requires intentional practice.

It is a journey of self-discovery and empowerment, where we reclaim control over our thoughts and emotions, liberating ourselves from the grip of our past conditioning. As we embrace this transformation, we become the architects of our destiny, designing a new path for ourselves with thoughts that elevate us and feelings that empower us. In this dance of mind and body, we discover the true essence of our being—a dynamic force of endless possibilities and growth.

I will share a few exercises for how to un-memorise unwanted feelings, thoughts, and behaviours and how to implement new ways of thinking and being. **You can find the exercise in the section called "Self-Coaching Practice" on page 173,** but first I would like to introduce how our brain works in a very basic way.

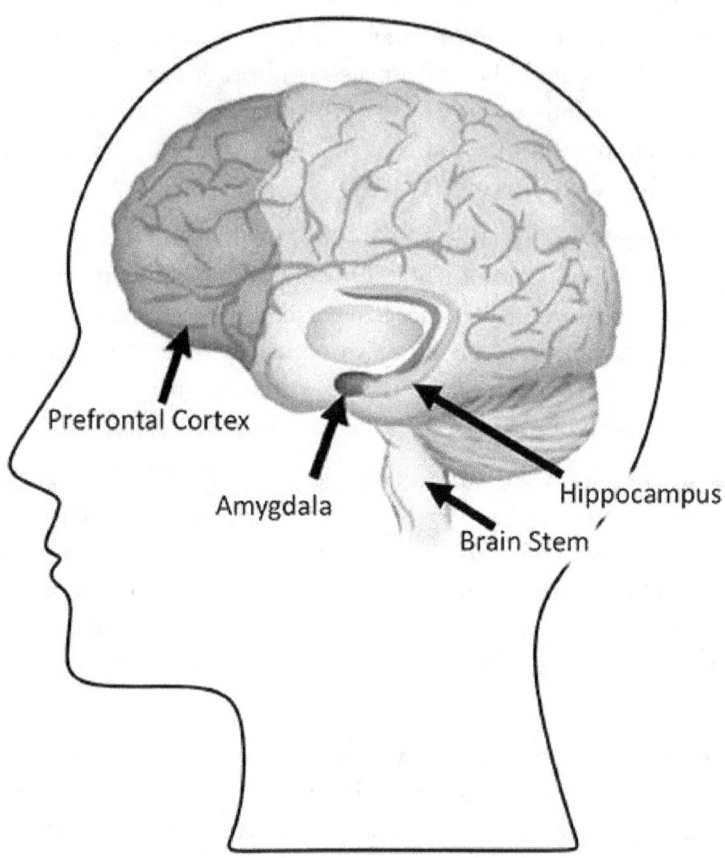

The frontal lobe—domain of creation and change

Creation mode is a state of complete engagement and flow, where the world around us fades away and time seems to lose its grip on us. It's those precious moments when we are fully immersed in something we truly love and enjoy, leaving no space for conscious thoughts about the environment or our physical bodies. It's as if we transcend the boundaries of time and space, becoming pure immaterial awareness. In this extraordinary state, we may connect with our true selves and experience profound transformation.

During creation mode, the brain's creative centre, known as the frontal lobe or prefrontal cortex, takes centre stage. This remarkable part of our nervous system is the most evolved and adaptable region of the brain. It serves as the CEO or decision-maker, responsible for our attention, focused concentration, awareness, observation, and firm intention. The frontal lobe governs conscious decisions, keeps impulsive and emotional behaviours in check, and facilitates our capacity to learn and grow.

If we desire to create a new version of ourselves, we must start by cultivating strong awareness and deeply understanding our old self. This requires stepping into the role of an observer, keenly observing all the subconscious behaviours and habits we wish to change. After all, we can only change what we are conscious of.

The frontal lobe plays a pivotal role in this process, as it empowers us to bring awareness to our old self and its patterns. By becoming observers of our own thoughts and actions, we lay the foundation for transformation. This journey of self-awareness and observation is the first step toward creating a new personality and embracing the limitless potential within us.

Create a new mind—new ways of being

The second function of the frontal lobe is to embark on the journey of creating a new mind. It all begins when we set aside a private, contemplative space to explore a fresh way of being. In this exercise, the frontal lobe comes alive, engaging in the process of creation. We open ourselves to new possibilities, envisioning a new personality, behaviours, and emotions. We ask ourselves profound questions:

- What do I truly desire?
- How do I want to be?
- What would it feel like to embody a different way of being?
- What do I want to embody?
- What is the new feeling I want to feel and experience daily?

We dive deeper into imagination, shaping our thoughts into a new reality.

The exercise later in this part called "Self-coaching practice" will guide you through this transformative process of observation, acceptance, and creation.

Now the third role of the frontal lobe comes into play—making thought more potent than anything else. In a state of creativity, the frontal lobe activates intensely, turning down the volume of other brain circuits. This singular focus allows our thoughts to become all-encompassing, surpassing the distractions of the external world. Our inner world of thoughts gains the power of reality, merging seamlessly with our external experiences.

As we engage in this creative process, our thoughts are imprinted into the architecture of our brains, becoming tangible experiences. Emotions are sparked, and we begin to feel as though the envisioned event is genuinely unfolding in the present moment. It's as if we are rewriting our subconscious programs, reconditioning our bodies to align with the new minds we are creating.

In this extraordinary journey of thought and emotion, we plant the seeds of transformation within ourselves. By harnessing the power of the frontal lobe and the creative force of our minds, we can pave the way to embrace a new reality, one that aligns with our deepest desires and aspirations. The process of creating a new mind is the gateway to limitless growth and expansion, unlocking the potential for profound change and self-discovery.

The two states of mind: survival versus creation

The two states of mind, survival and creation, represent contrasting ways of experiencing and navigating life.

Survival mode is a state where our thoughts and actions are primarily focused on immediate threats and challenges. It's a reactive state, driven by fear and aimed at ensuring our basic needs and safety are met. In survival mode, we are constantly on guard, seeking to avoid potential dangers and protect ourselves from harm. This state is often associated with stress, anxiety, pressure, and a sense of urgency.

On the other hand, creation mode is a state of active engagement and growth. It's a proactive state, fuelled by inspiration and vision. In creation mode, we are open to possibilities, seeking to explore and expand our potential. We are driven by a sense of purpose and a desire to bring something new and meaningful into existence. This state is characterised by passion, enthusiasm, flow and a sense of fulfilment.

While survival mode is essential for dealing with immediate challenges and threats, it can become limiting if we stay stuck in this state for prolonged periods. It may lead to a narrow focus on survival needs, preventing us from fully embracing opportunities for growth and self-discovery.

Creation mode, on the other hand, allows us to tap into our creativity and innovation. It encourages us to dream big, set goals, and take inspired action. In this state, we are more likely to overcome obstacles and turn challenges into stepping stones for growth.

The key to living a fulfilling life is to strike a balance between survival and creation modes. While survival mode helps us address urgent needs and protect ourselves, creation mode empowers us to envision a better future and take deliberate steps towards realising our dreams.

By consciously cultivating creation mode, we can unlock our potential and create a life that aligns with our deepest aspirations.

The three brains

From thinking and doing to being

The human brain is a remarkable organ with three distinct regions that shape our experiences and behaviours—the neocortex, the limbic brain, and the cerebellum.

The **neocortex**, often referred to as the **thinking brain**, is the outer layer of the brain and represents the most advanced neurological hardware in humanity. It houses the conscious mind and is responsible for higher brain functions such as decision-making, problem-solving, and abstract thinking. The neocortex allows us to process complex information and envision possibilities that we have not yet experienced. It serves as the seat of our identity, shaping our sense of self and how we perceive the world around us.

Beneath the neocortex lies the **limbic brain,** a highly developed area found in mammals other than humans, such as dolphins and higher primates. Think of the limbic brain as the **emotional brain,** the centre where our emotions and feelings originate. This intricate region plays a crucial role in shaping our emotional responses and motivations. When we encounter new experiences or stimuli, our senses send a rush of information to the neocortex, and its neural networks organise themselves to reflect the event. This process enriches the brain beyond mere knowledge, turning it into a true learning experience that involves both the conscious and emotional realms.

In the class or group coaching environment, we not only gain knowledge but also engage in practical exercises that allow us to practise and integrate the tools and concepts presented. By doing so, we create profound and memorable experiences that involve both our thoughts and emotions. Emotions play a vital role here, as they signal genes in new ways, chemically recording the event in our bodies and helping form long-term memories. When we can recall how we felt emotionally during the learning experience, we can better remember and internalise the knowledge and skills acquired.

Moving from thinking and doing to being is a transformative process that involves the cerebellum, the most active part of the brain, located at the back of the skull. The cerebellum is often seen as the brain's processor and memory centre. It plays a significant role in the formation of habits, conditioned behaviours, and unconscious reflexes that we have mastered and memorised through practice and repetition. When we practise and repeat certain actions or skills, they become ingrained in our subconscious, leading to a state of being where these behaviours become almost automatic.

Additionally, the **amygdala**, nestled in the middle of the brain, is another crucial player in shaping our emotions and behaviours. The amygdala is associated with processing emotions and memories, particularly those linked to fear and pleasure. It is part of the limbic system, which is essential for emotional regulation and understanding our emotional responses.

Understanding the basic functions of the brain provides profound insights into how we can change our minds and transform our lives. By harnessing the power of our neocortex and limbic brain, we can shape our personalities, develop emotional intelligence, and unlock our full potential for growth and self-discovery. **Through continuous learning, practice, and self-awareness, we can create a harmonious connection between our thoughts, emotions, and actions, leading to a fulfilling and purposeful life.**

Here is an exercise to change the old you and create a better version of yourself.

Self-coaching practice

Let's start a transformative journey of awareness, acknowledgement, acceptance, observation, and creation as we dive into the depths of our emotions and beliefs to effect positive change in our lives. This chapter was inspired by my mentor and teacher, Dr Joe Dispenza, who uses a lot of techniques based on neuroscience and the practice of meditation to transform people's lives. I absolutely love his work and he has been my daily inspiration for the past decade.

Okay, let's start:

Awareness. Begin by understanding what aspects of your old self you want to change. Let your frontal lobe, the thinking brain, guide you through self-reflection with these probing questions. Simply write down the answers; don't overthink them:

- Who have I been up until now?
- How do I present myself to the world?
- What kind of person am I inside?
- Do I struggle with a specific emotion daily?
- How would my closest friends and family describe me?
- Is there a part of myself that I hide from others and don't want to be seen?
- Which aspects of my personality need improvement?
- What is the one thing I truly want to change about myself?

Acknowledgement. Embrace your true self and acknowledge any limitations you found without judgement. Allow yourself to explore these acknowledgements and seek resolution. For example:

- I sometimes lie to gain acceptance and avoid feeling unloved and unworthy.
- I hide my guilt by pretending to be someone else.

Acceptance. Let go of self-limiting beliefs and surrender them to a greater mind, asking for resolution in the way that best serves you.

Observation. Take a moment to observe your automatic thoughts when experiencing the unwanted emotion you identified. Recognise patterns and replace them with positive affirmations, like:

- I am capable of finding a new job.
- People value what I have to say.
- I choose to respond positively to difficult situations.

Now, contemplate how you habitually act when feeling the unwanted emotion:

- Instead of sulking, I will address my emotions constructively.
- I will refrain from overeating when feeling down.
- I will seek to communicate openly and calmly about my feelings.

Creation. Reflect on the following questions and explore the potential for positive change:

- What is my greatest ideal?
- How would it feel to embody that ideal?
- Who in history do I admire, and how did they act?
- Do I know someone in my life who embodies the qualities I seek to adopt?
- How can I think more like the person I aspire to be?
- Whose behaviour do I want to model?
- If I were transformed, how would I act differently?
- What encouraging words would I tell myself as this new version of me?
- How would my interactions with others change?
- What reminders or cues can I use to maintain this new mindset?

Through identifying our current state, acknowledging and approving our true selves, surrendering limiting beliefs and self-concept, and embracing a new creation, we unlock the power within us to change and grow, stepping into a life of purpose and self-actualisation.

Choose how you want to think!

How would I like to think?

- What would my ideal self's thought patterns be like?
- Which thoughts do I want to channel my energy into?
- What attitude will reflect my new mindset?
- What empowering beliefs do I want to cultivate about myself?
- What encouraging words would I speak to myself as this transformed person?

How do I wish to behave?

- How will this new version of myself act?
- What actions and behaviours would they demonstrate?
- How do I see my redefined self behaving in various situations?
- What language and tone would I adopt as this improved expression of self?

How do I aspire to feel?

- How will this evolved self experience emotions?
- What emotions will I feel in this new state of being?

Create a new destiny—imagine your ideal future, having achieved your desired goals and vision. Describe everything as if it is already happening in the present moment. Fill in all the details of this envisioned reality.

How do you exercise your brain?

To create a better brain, we need to take care of it. It's the same thing as going to the gym. We need to start going to the brain gym!

It would be very helpful for your brain health, longevity, creativity, memory, and positive psychology to exercise your brain daily for at least five minutes. Remember, you are what you eat. Feed your brain with good stuff.

Here are some ideas to implement:

Cold therapy. We know to apply ice to reduce swelling; it lowers inflammation in your body, resets your nervous system, calms you down, relaxes you, puts you in a state of creativity and awareness and encourages new ideas.

Hydrate. Our body contains 70% water—we need to hydrate for better brain functions; dehydration leads to brain fog. You can use some herbs like gotu kola, ginkgo biloba, MCT (medium-chain triglycerides), and honey—these activate your focus.

Dreams. Try to remember your dreams as soon as you wake up.

Journalling. Successful artists, architects, and athletes keep journals, write, and reflect. I have a very specific process of journalling, but what I can mention is to have one list or one book for ideas for the future, because these come to our mind and brain every day and we can be easily distracted by new ideas—the shiny object—but we need to stay focused on the thing we're doing right now and get results first. Then we can keep these ideas in another book or journal and we can come back to them later. I also recommend having a *not*-to-do list!

A lot of effective people have a not-to-do list—for example, in the first hour after you wake up, don't touch your phone, because it will distract you. It trains you to be reactive! What if you get a bad message or email and that puts you in a bad mood? Why would you do that to yourself?

Add three things to your journal. Add your top three priorities to win the day. Make a decision about what you will do today and what your day will look like—what you want to cover personally and professionally.

Nutrition. Choose great nutrition for your brain—MCT oil, avocado, greens, blueberries, power smoothies, coconut oil, broccoli, salmon, sardines, turmeric, walnuts, and carrots. Dark chocolate is the best for increasing endorphins!

Read something every day. Read one book a week!

Exercise. Of course, we know exercise sends positive hormones to our body and makes us feel happier.

Breathing techniques. My favourite. I love to take a deep, conscious breath a few times a day. Focus on your breath. Take a deep, loud inhale through your nose, hold for ten or twenty seconds, breathe out loud through your mouth, and repeat at least five times. You will feel amazing and you will gain new energy and create more energy in your brain cells.

The brain is the most important organ in our body, and yet we don't really focus on training and taking care of our brain. Our thinking, our brain, and the correct hormonal balance are important foundations for our emotional state, happiness, and resilience.

The 9 building blocks for resilience and longevity

1. **Make connections.** Good relationships with close family members, friends, or others are important. Accept help and support from those who care about you and will listen to you to strengthen your resilience. Some people find that being active in civic groups, faith-based organisations, or other local groups provides social support and can help with reclaiming hope. Assisting others in their time of need can also benefit the helper.

2. **Reframe your perspective on crises.** While it's true that challenging and stressful events are inevitable, you have the power to alter how you perceive and handle them. Instead of viewing them as insurmountable obstacles, try to envision a future where circumstances improve, even if only slightly. Take note of any subtle shifts in your emotions or outlook that may occur as you navigate tough situations. By doing so, you can find glimmers of hope and progress amidst the difficulties.

3. **Accept that change is a part of living.** Certain goals may no longer be attainable as a result of adverse situations. Accepting circumstances that cannot be changed can help you focus on circumstances that you can alter.

4. **Move toward your goals.** Develop some realistic goals. Do something regularly—even if it seems like a small accomplishment—that enables you to move toward your goals. Instead of focusing on tasks that seem unachievable, ask yourself, "What's one thing I know I can accomplish today that helps me move in the direction I want to go?"

5. **Take decisive actions.** Act on adverse situations as much as you can. Take decisive actions, rather than detaching completely from problems and stresses and wishing they would just go away.

6. **Look for opportunities for self-discovery.** People often learn something about themselves and may find that they have grown in some respect as a result of their struggle with loss. Many people who have experienced tragedies and hardship have reported better relationships, a greater sense of strength even while feeling vulnerable, an increased sense of self-worth, a more developed spirituality, and a heightened appreciation for life.

7. **Nurture a positive view and thoughts of yourself.** Developing confidence in your ability to solve problems and trusting your instincts helps build resilience.

8. **Keep things in perspective.** Even when facing very painful events, try to consider the stressful situation in a broader context and keep a long-term perspective. Avoid blowing the event out of proportion.

9. **Take care of yourself.** Pay attention to your own needs and feelings. Engage in activities that you enjoy and find relaxing. Exercise regularly. Taking care of yourself helps to keep your mind and body primed to deal with situations that require resilience.

We are a collective species that has evolved over billions of years. From our origins as a bacterium to a society that now has the ability to consciously reflect, over time we have continuously developed into something more advanced. The evolution of our brains and nervous system over this time has indeed built the ability to feel a wide array of emotions.

In those emotions, humans have landed on the capacity to create a meaningful and fulfilling life through happiness, and we have also been able to evolve our understanding of happiness over time, from as far back as the fourth century BCE.

As our understanding of happiness has also evolved, we can now implement, as a society, changes that will benefit us all greatly. Through steps taken towards "positive psychology", we can continue to evolve into a happier and more well-balanced society.

Behaviour —connection and communication

The Behavioural level in the CEB method for leadership refers to the tangible actions, habits, and patterns of behaviour that leaders or team members exhibit in their day-to-day interactions.

It encompasses the practical aspects of leadership and focuses on implementing changes in real-life situations. Here's what should be covered at the Behavioural level and why it is essential:

Processes and systems. This involves the establishment and optimisation of effective processes and systems in your day-to-day life or within the organisation. Leaders or business owners need to ensure that the right structures are in place, workflows are efficient, and there is clarity in roles and responsibilities. Well-defined processes contribute to better coordination, increased productivity, and smoother operations.

Habits and routines. Habits play a significant role in shaping our behaviour. People, especially leaders, must identify and cultivate positive habits that align with their goals and the organisation's vision. By consistently practising positive habits, leaders can model the behaviour they expect from their team and create a culture of excellence.

Reward system: The neuroscience of reward and the dopamine system are indeed crucial in behavioural change. Leaders should design a reward system that recognises and reinforces desired behaviours. This could include praise, conversations, recognition, promotions, or even financial incentives based on collective effort. A well-structured reward system not only motivates employees to excel but also helps them maintain high levels of engagement and stay aligned with their values. A reward system depends on industry, personality, and team dynamics.

Communication. Effective and mindful communication is the backbone of successful relationships, leadership, and life in general. Every person should focus on honing their communication skills, both verbal and non-verbal, to build trust and inspire confidence in their family, community, or team. Clear and transparent communication fosters a positive environment and minimises misunderstandings.

Decision-making. Leaders need to cultivate sound decision-making skills. This involves gathering relevant information, considering different perspectives, and making well-informed choices. Leaders who can make wise decisions under pressure are more likely to lead their teams to success.

Respond and react—emotional intelligence. Emotional intelligence is vital for leaders to understand and manage their own emotions and those of others. It enables leaders to navigate challenging situations, build strong relationships, and respond empathetically to the needs of their team.

Conflict resolution. Leaders should be equipped with conflict resolution skills to address conflicts that may arise among team members or in the workplace. The ability to handle conflicts constructively promotes a harmonious work environment and improves team dynamics.

The Behavioural level in the CEB method focuses on the practical implementation of cognitive and emotional changes in the real world. By addressing processes, habits, reward systems, communication, and other behavioural aspects, leaders can create a positive and productive work environment, drive behavioural change, and achieve their leadership objectives.

Now, to assess these three levels and approach them as a leader, we need to be aware that our role is not only being a boss or someone who guides people towards one united vision. We have so many other roles as a leader.

A leader's roles

In my opinion, the role of a leader is not that of a commander or someone solely focused on checking off tasks. To me, a leader is more of a **facilitator**, someone who nurtures and empowers the talent within the team and fosters an environment of growth, progress and facilitates high performance and outstanding results. They possess a grand vision that guides the team towards their goals and can realign us when we stray from the intended path.

What sets an inspiring leader apart is their ability to ignite passion and motivation in others through their infectious energy, unwavering drive, honesty, and captivating visions. They genuinely care about their team members, going above and beyond to ensure the fulfilment of the team's purpose. Their influence is so compelling that we are eager to learn and aspire to be like them.

A remarkable leader draws us in with their authenticity, humanity, and love. They exemplify the virtues of great leadership, leading with integrity, empathy, and a deep understanding of the people they lead. Their ability to connect on a personal level makes us feel valued, heard, and supported.

The leader I admire is a facilitator of greatness, an inspiring force who guides us towards our goals and nurtures our talents. They create an atmosphere of trust and collaboration, making us feel valued and motivated to achieve more. Their vision and care for the team, combined with their magnetic qualities, make them an extraordinary leader we all aspire to emulate.

Let's have a look at what roles as a leader we can think of.

Leader as a guide. We are ultimately there to guide our team members through their personal and career journey of exploration. We are there to assist the team members to experience their journey with more ease, growth, and positive experiences. We are here to understand their strengths and help them to understand their strengths, stretches, and opportunities. Show them the bigger picture, which includes their vision, values, higher purpose, and their reason for being in the team.

Leader as facilitator. We are shining a torch on the path ahead so they don't get caught up in the distractions, processes, and noise that would pull them away from the vision or mission and ultimate goal.

We are here to facilitate a great, healthy, and balanced environment where people can thrive, grow, contribute, and innovate. We are here to facilitate a safe place where people feel heard, seen, and understood. The leader can play the role of collaborator, providing the team with someone to brainstorm possibilities with. They should not just tell the team what to do but should instead facilitate open conversations where everyone collaborates and shares ideas without being right because of the position.

Leader as inspirer. Our team members are approaching and experimenting with new ideas and possibilities. We become experts at ideas that are fundamentally sustainable—they are true in all environments and in all situations. We can show people new perceptions and ideas; for example, the idea that love is fundamental to self-worth. We demonstrate values and we help them to open their minds to see more possibilities for their growth and fulfilment.

Leader as challenger. Everything we do is a strategy. Every action, choice, decision—everything we do—is a strategy that will produce a specific outcome. If we run our strategy the same way, we will achieve the same result. If we want a different result, we must change our strategy. The leader can challenge a strategy that is not effective or is resulting in an outcome that is not aligned with where the team members said they wanted to be. The leader can simply reflect back to the team members what they're observing. This mirror reflection provides the team members with the opportunity for personal reflection to decide if what they've expressed is, in fact, what they intended or what they really mean.

As leaders, we should be able to notice and reflect back to the client patterns we observe that we can see will not benefit them—ones that will take them away from their goal.

Chapter 7

Effective and Influential Communication

To me, effective and influential communication is one of the most important soft skills or behaviours that needs to be learnt and nurtured.

Effective and influential communication to me is mindful communication. It is the art of connecting with others in a genuine, present, and empathetic manner. It involves being fully engaged and attentive when interacting with people, whether through spoken words, body language, or facial expressions.

Mindful communication goes beyond the surface level of exchanging information; it seeks to understand and connect on a deeper level, acknowledging emotions, thoughts, and feelings.

I believe that mindful communication is the number one skill of leadership and influence because, as social creatures, our ability to connect with others is fundamental to our success in any group or organisation.

From the very beginning, when we interact with even just one other person, we are already communicating through subtle body energies, nonverbal cues, and micro-expressions that we may not consciously notice, but unconsciously, we sense and respond to them. These subtle signals can significantly impact how others perceive us and how we build relationships.

That's why we are working on the thinking, emotional, and behavioural levels (CEB) to create understanding and change on all levels to be perceived as a great influencer and communicator consciously and subconsciously.

Mindful communication is essential in leadership because it fosters trust, respect, and understanding among team members. When leaders actively listen and show genuine interest in the concerns and perspectives of their team, they create a safe and open environment where everyone feels heard and valued. This, in turn, boosts team morale, encourages collaboration, and enhances productivity. Mindful communication is one of the most important aspects of creating psychological safety and high performance.

As a leader, I believe in the power of mindful communication because it allows us to truly connect with others, inspiring them to be their best selves. By practising mindfulness and being present in our interactions, we can build stronger relationships, motivate our team, and lead by example. Mindful communication helps us avoid misunderstandings, conflicts, and misinterpretations, enabling us to navigate challenges more effectively and create a positive and supportive work culture.

I consider effective mindful communication to be the cornerstone of successful business, leadership, and influence because we are inherently communicators, and our ability to connect authentically and empathetically with others is crucial in achieving shared goals and fostering a thriving, harmonious environment. It is through mindful communication that we can lead with compassion, inspire others, and create a lasting impact on those around us.

How to communicate effectively?

Effective communication skills are fundamental to success in many aspects of life. I believe these are four key areas for improvement and building influential communication skills:

- Listening
- Body language
- Emotional awareness
- Questioning.

I was shocked to discover that words represent only around 7% of what influences our behaviour. Voice and tonality represent around 38% of what influences us. So, how we use our voice affects someone more than what we say.

Another part of communication is physiology or body language, representing 55%. The way we use our bodies, muscles, and facial expressions represents the majority of what actually influences people when we communicate.

To put it another way, the song we hear (communication) is made up of the lyrics (words), tune (tonality), and rhythm (body language). How often have you loved the beat of a song but you don't care much for the lyrics? The song still gets to you!

What's remarkable about this is that it tells us what we say can be undermined by how we say it or how we move our bodies. We can communicate one thing with words, but the listener detects an entirely different message. If we don't believe what we are saying, people notice that. That's why we can't explain why we don't trust some people—they are not authentic. How many times have you spoken with a salesperson and known they didn't believe in the product or service they were selling or have said things you know from their expression aren't true?

Foundation of influence—rapport

Creating rapport with someone is not guesswork. It is simply a matter of discovering the meaning that the other person gives to their world and reflecting it back to them. One of the key techniques for this is to match and mirror as you communicate. You can build rapport by matching:

- Physiology
- Voice/language
- Representational system
- Beliefs
- Experience
- Breathing.

Take your time in the conversation. Don't fill in silences. Don't rush to say the word they're thinking of. Let them find their way with you and match them.

The impact of active listening

Be present:

- Great eye contact
- Staying still
- Mirroring/matching
- Being curious
- Active listening—don't plan what you will say in response to someone else in front of you

How to be present:

- Listen generously
- Listen for patterns and meaning
- Listen without judgement
- Listen without assumptions

Ways to respond that demonstrate that we are being present:

- "Thank you"
- "That sounds important to you"
- "Hmmm"
- "Tell me more"
- "What else?"
- With silence

Exercise: Active Listening

Each person has seven minutes to talk about any achievements, issues, solutions, innovations, or adventures—work or life-related—they like. When listening, observe all three things: being present, how you managed to be present, and what responses you used to help the other person open up and feel great and supported.

Imagine words don't have meaning. The only meaning we put into words is through our perception. Try to listen beyond the words. It is a very new concept but focuses on what is really going on in the person's world. Not in your world, not what you think about the words or person. Just come to the conversation open, with no judgement.

Body language

Body language actually covers far more than just your posture. It includes tone, gestures, eye contact, pitch of the voice, body movement, facial expression, and even psychological changes such as sweating or skin colour changes. If we were able to notice all of those signs, we could understand other people better by paying attention to their non-verbal communication.

Positive body language:

What is positive body language?

People find positive language appealing, receptive, and easy to confront. Positive body language must place us in a position of comfort, dignity, and likeability. It helps us to be open to other people and be approachable, helping them feel comfortable when they are interacting with us. If our body movements somehow convey the opposite, then our body language is not positive and hence, needs to be improved.

Body language must not be defensive. Defensive body language discourages people from approaching us and establishing a connection with us.

Body language must not display a sense of disinterest towards the other person, as it can lead to failure in jobs, interviews, and high-profile meetings.

The body language of a person must neither be authoritative nor submissive, but assertive to put forth our opinion and stance confidently without meaning any offence to the other person.

Every day we interact and build relationships with everyone we meet. Have you ever considered why you just click with some people and others you just don't and why we, ourselves, think and act in a certain way? It all boils down to our own subconscious mind, past experiences, and memories. Often, we unconsciously judge people based on these past experiences, even before giving them a chance to reveal their true selves. Therefore, allow yourself to approach each conversation without judgment, personal opinions, or pre-formed perspectives. Take the time to truly get to know someone and understand their intentions.

Questions for effective communication

Questioning is a crucial skill to ensure that you have understood someone's message correctly.

It is also a very good way of obtaining more information about a particular topic or simply starting a conversation and keeping it going. Those with good questioning skills are often also seen as very good listeners, because they tend to spend far more time drawing information out from others rather than broadcasting their own opinions. This is a very crucial skill for leaders and I would suggest focusing on building your repertoire of questions and frameworks which will help you to listen, mentor, coach, and help people to grow. You will be able to shift their thinking and perceptions and also create an internal sense of inspiration.

When we ask great questions, we set a framework that allows exploration, discovery, transformation, and empowerment. They will drive the conversation in a certain way. They will cause other conversations to not happen. They will determine our focus, our energy, and our thoughts.

We will go through a few major models for training, implementing, and building your questioning skills. But let's start with a major step and skill we need to build up when we first start to communicate.

Calibration

Calibration is the ability to tune into another person and what level of energy, conversational pace, movement, and attitude they are choosing to operate with at that moment. When you match and mirror the person in front of you, you will constantly calibrate the nuances of these aspects and adjust your own energy, conversational pace, movement, and attitude to match that person.

The leader, as a coach and mentor, must calibrate the client to determine what non-verbal and verbal signals they are communicating.

If we're not paying attention, we may hear the person say, "That's great," and be done with it.

What we didn't observe was the person sighing and looking away with a frown.

While we can't know for sure, it's worth at least asking, "Is there something else to look at here?"

We may discover that their agreement was because they didn't want to let us down rather than their own desire to do the thing. To calibrate our team members, we must utilise what's called *sensory acuity*. Sensory acuity is the ability to notice the minute movements the other person is showing us from moment to moment if we're paying attention.

We don't assign meaning to the movements. If we assume we know what the movements or sounds mean, we're doing what's called "mind reading" or "hallucinating". We're assigning meaning to what we observe without checking in.

So we ask:

"Did something just happen then?"

"Hmmm. Something just came up for you. Would you mind sharing?"

"I see that the question raises other stuff for you. Great. I'm wondering what that may be."

We may notice:

- Forehead may raise/lifting eyebrows
- Colour change
- Lips parted or lips pressed together
- Eyes watering
- Sighing
- A shift in the seat for a small moment.

None of these movements are necessarily significant. Just ask. If they're not, the person will tell you.

Physiology

Body posture and movement

People who get on well together tend to adopt the same body posture when communicating. They use similar gestures and mannerisms.

Look for things like:
- Body posture and position
- Leg position
- The angle they rest their body
- Repeated patterns of movement with hands or feet
- The pace at which they drink.

Voice

Tone, speed of speech, and other voice characteristics

Notice the:
- Tempo
- Volume
- Pitch
- Tone
- Rhythm
- Phrases and timbre they use.

Beliefs and values

What people hold true and important

Match the other person's values and beliefs by showing an acknowledgement of them. For example, if someone values time, then a comment that would be appropriate would be "I wouldn't want to waste your time," or "How can we make the best use of this time?"

Experience

Finding common ground

Establish common ground in interests and activities. This applies even to simple observations such as the weather or the traffic.

What would be appropriate responses to the following comments?

- I like sunny days.
- It's warm today.
- I always make my decisions quickly.
- I learnt about computers at school.
- I am married.

Breathing

As you develop your sensory acuity, you will notice that we even breathe in different ways. Matching breathing patterns is a subtle way of building rapport.

How do you establish and maintain rapport?

There are so many ways to maintain rapport. Most significantly, don't make it about you. It's all about them!

You can also:

Continue to match and mirror them throughout the conversation and use comments that are artfully vague:

- "Hmm …"
- "I see …"
- "How does that work?"
- "For what purpose?"
- "All the things we're looking at are here for us to see …"
- "It's a good thing we know the signs …"

- "You like that, don't you?"

Have sensory acuity and calibrate it to the person in front of you. If they are uptight, match it with your body and maybe not match it with your words (crossover matching).

If they are too relaxed, you can bring them back up to awareness by being specific with your language, by saying, "How specifically?" or "What is it about your beliefs that led you to choose that?"

Pacing and leading

Pacing and leading are used to test rapport and to effect transformation once rapport is established. Pacing is matching and mirroring the behaviours, and leading is moving the other person forward or towards something.

For example, a client who is apprehensive may be leaning back with their arms folded. The coach would match this behaviour by sitting with their arms folded initially and then gradually start moving towards more open gestures (unfolding arms, sitting forward, and so forth). If the other person follows the coach, the coach knows that they have a rapport and have moved the client into a more receptive frame.

Pacing and leading means matching and mirroring and then moving forward.

Matching can also apply when dealing with someone who feels angry or negative. First pace (match) their behaviour, within reason, and then lead them to your (and probably their) outcome.

Effective listening skills

I was always that person who wanted to say something quickly in each conversation. I realised I was so focused on what I would say the next that I missed so many great conversations or the deeper meaning of those conversations. When I listened to Sydney Banks and his Hawaiian lectures, I was so annoyed by his words that I wanted to give up the whole course, but then he said, "If those words make you angry, you are not listening. Listen beyond words." Ah, this got me. I experienced such a shift in my thinking and perceiving or projecting. But most importantly, I experienced a massive shift in listening and I just cried for the next hour. I know it sounds weird, but when we go through shifts and transformational moments, we get an emotional release and a deeper connection to something beyond us. And this is listening.

We each have the ability to listen at the level needed to create the space needed for transformation to occur. We need to remember that the simple act of observation will impact the outcomes. To observe without 100% focus will not serve your team member or friend.

Effective listeners:

- are present
- concentrate on the speaker or on their voice
- respond to what the speaker has said
- make a response that is relevant to what the speaker has said
- ask questions to check their understanding
- make comments (and agreement) without interrupting the speaker
- make notes if needed
- evaluate what they are hearing
- remain alert through good body language (posture particularly)
- allow the speaker's conversation to flow
- notice the person's modality
- notice their tonality, body language, chunk levels, and so on.

Being present includes:

- great eye contact
- staying still and practising active listening
- nodding to encourage
- mirroring/matching
- being curious
- listening generously
- listening for patterns and meaning

- listening without judgement
- listening without assumptions.

Ways to respond when we are present:

- "Thank you"
- "That sounds important to you"
- "Tell me more"
- "What else?"
- With silence

Listen generously

- Focus completely on the person. If you notice yourself drifting, then bring your mind and focus back to the person in front of you. When they know you are listening completely, they feel acknowledged and valued.
- Listen with empathy. Regardless of how you would do things in their situation, it is important that you recognise that they are doing the best they can with the resources that they have.
- Listen without interrupting. Don't ever finish their sentence for them.

Listen for patterns

Everyone does what they do because on some level it is working for them. Your job as a coach is to listen for these patterns in behaviour and choices.

Notice if they respond to certain events in a similar way and share this with them. Help bring awareness to their patterns, especially if you have one team member who is demonstrating procrastination, anger, or frustration. This is a very good example because you, as a leader and as a coach, should be able to recognise what is stopping or limiting the other person and when that usually happens.

Notice their values and the beliefs that seem to recur. This is my favourite topic because we all have some limiting beliefs and limitations that get in the way of the success or outcome we want. It is great if you, as a leader, can recognise what is stopping and limiting the other person and then share that insight with them.

Listen beyond the words and be careful to not make assumptions about what they could mean.

Listen without judgement

This is never about you. This is their journey and it is important that you see it that way. Avoid reacting emotionally or with your opinions. This is not about you.

If you are coming from a place of judgement, you can notice that you already judge the outcome or what that person says. It's like you are a mind reader. Or you already judge the situation and create anxiety about the upcoming conversation. Or you may notice your heart rate is going up or you are getting a bit irritated or even angry. This happens when we are coming from a place of judgement. Take a few breaths to calm yourself down and approach the conversation from a space of acceptance, understanding, and love.

Clarifying

To clear the space for the speaker, we suspend judgement and opinion. Simply reflect what you are hearing and sensing. By doing this, we allow the speaker to fill the space with their truth.

For example:

- What I'm hearing is frustration because you're not getting the outcome you wanted. Is this right?
- What I'm sensing is that you're really clear about what you want to do, but unsure about how. Is that right?
- What I'm seeing is confusion about the best choice to act on. Is that right?

Remember, this is about the speaker finding out for themselves what their truth is rather than you giving them your answer.

Acknowledging

True acknowledgement recognises the core of who the person is. It can help someone see what they may dismiss through a lack of confidence or because of humility.

By acknowledging a person's strength, you give them the power to access it. One of the benefits of this is that, in future, that person will tap into that quality more readily, thus building the foundation for even more growth. Another benefit is that you have built rapport with someone effortlessly, thus fostering the relationship.

Action exercise:

Acknowledge someone (your team member or colleague) for their work or for behaviour you really admire and you want to see more at your workplace. What to acknowledge can be attitude, behaviour, an achievement, a new skill, an achieved result, innovation, or even when they try something new, living by core values, displaying humour or courage, or being willing to mess up.

Questions to avoid

There are types of questions that we can avoid in order to maintain effective communication. The following types of questions lead the participant to shut down. These questions are not about exploration or curiosity but are considered to be "labelling".

Why?

- "Why did you do that?"
- "Why are you telling me this?"
- "Why can't I?"

These types of questions invariably leave the participant defending and justifying their choices. When someone defends the way things are, they are unlikely to want to give this position up.

It's difficult to coach someone who is in the bunker, defending themselves with reasons and justifications.

Closed questions

These questions only have two responses: yes or no. In this frame of mind, the person in front of us doesn't need to think. They isolate and create no interest in continuing the conversation.

This type of question isolates the person from their consciousness.

- "Did you do it?"
- "Can you do it?"
- "Are you going to do it?"
- "Am I right?"
- "Do you agree?"

Also, avoid multiple questions in one sentence. When asking questions, come from a place of:

- Curiosity about the person
- A passion to assist
- A willingness to check in that you are on the same track
- Planting seeds.

See the road ahead and plant seeds about what it might take to traverse the road you see:

- "This will take courage, so how will you prepare for being stretched?"
- "This is about you being ready to live to your full potential. How will you know you are doing that?

Evoking discovery

If you see an obvious connection, let your client notice it too. Encourage playful discovery.

Don't be overly attached to any one idea, because plenty will come and go and it's about your willingness to dance and attach lightly to ideas rather than be convinced this is the one true path. Let go of this attachment to everything and notice how much stronger your coaching becomes.

Challenge

Don't let limits stand. Don't accept the limits, even if in your own mind you think they could be valid. Your coaching truly opens up when you have an attitude that "anything is possible; we just haven't found how *yet*". Challenge every limit, unresourceful comment, blind spot, and story you hear. Be a brave leader, because they need you to be brave so they can see it's possible for themselves, too. Be the leader they want to be.

The art of questions

I am sure you have already heard that if you are looking for high-quality answers and results you need to ask high-quality questions.

To me, questions lead to answers and create results. That's why I decided to share a few different ways of seeing and using questions. You can increase your and others' awareness by asking the right questions. You can gain more clarity or fire up the imagination.

You can use these questions for self-coaching or coaching others.

Awareness questions

These questions help us to see what "is". For something to change, we first must see it for what it is. These questions assist us in observing and seeing our world for what it is, free of judgement or evaluation. We simply notice the experience.

For example, "When you think about doing that, what do you feel inside you?"

Clarifying questions

These questions seek to clarify with the client what something means to them in terms of importance, significance, concern, and so on.

For example:
- For what purpose?
- How much?
- How important is it?
- To what extent?
- Tell me more ….
- How often?

Presuppositional questions:

"How can we turn this around?" presupposes that it *can* be turned around.

- "How is this working for you?"
- "How does this get resolved?"
- "What is the one thing that you need to see here to enable you to move forward?"

If you look throughout this manual, you will see presuppositions built into many of the questions.

What are three examples of presuppositional questions you can think of?

Inductive questions

Creative questions are designed to fire up our imagination. It's the difference between exploring what *is* (deductive) and exploring what *could be* (inductive).

Inductive questions take us to new territory and explore the dark holes between what we perceive to be real. They serve to open us up to what we haven't considered, haven't noticed, or haven't registered as important.

Examples include:
- What haven't you considered yet?
- Does it have to be this? What if it wasn't?
- If this didn't exist, what would there be instead?

- Go back in time before this challenge. What was going on?
- How can we approach this differently?

For what purpose gets clients to understand the bigger picture and to explore why things might be important to them.

For example:

- "For what purpose will you go for the interview?"
- "For what purpose do you want the job?"

Other **purpose** questions:

- "What would that give you?"
- "What's the positive intention of that?"
- "What's the ultimate intention of this?"

"Keep it real" questions

Questions that move the person towards their core purpose, instead of staying caught up in the noise of now, are helpful:

- "How can we turn this around?"
- "What would someone who had done this do?"
- "How do we nail this one so we can move to the next level?"
- "What's awesome about this?"

"Laser" questions

Laser questions are questions that get to the heart of what is really going on. Laser questions involve calling it as we see it.

Example of laser questions:

- "How is that belief going to support you?"
- "How are you limiting yourself right now?"
- "How are you hiding right now?"
- "Is it going to get you to move from here?"

- "What do you need to get unstuck?"
- "How's that working out?"

or

- "How can I support you?"
- "What do you need to do differently, so it moves you closer to how you want it to be?"

Now, you may ask, why did I dedicate a few chapters to communication? I'm a big believer that **mindful and open communication is a driver of positive change.** I believe when people start to communicate authentically with kindness and good intentions, they will not only create growth within themselves but will also help other people to grow through ongoing feedback and conversations. Mastering communication is mastering your voice and presenting yourself the way you want. It is a technique to get the message out there and cut through the noise. At the same time, active listening will help you to connect, collaborate, and influence others.

Chapter 8

Behaviours and Reprogramming Your Language

BAD THINGS ARE NOT ALWAYS THAT BAD, RIGHT?

Behaviours are learnt. Behaviours are something we do. They are how we conduct ourselves. Behaviours are the result of our thinking patterns and emotional state. Communication is a very big part of it because communication such as tonality, body language, and spoken language is something very obvious that people can notice and judge you upon. Communication gives clues. That's why bringing awareness to our communication patterns and mastering communication and language are the most important concepts to create a change. Language is a very powerful tool. How you speak to yourself also plays a big role. It is programming your mind and creating emotions within and therefore influencing your actions and behaviour. So, language is the number one tool or shortcut to reprogram the brain and behaviours. Language has a massive influence on your thinking and emotions. We feel how we speak and we speak how we feel.

So, I will give you an example. If you describe an event or tell me a story about a person and you are using words such as *horrible*, *hate*, *I can't*, and so on, I can guess that you are very angry with that person, that event traumatised you, or you are truly full of anger. The major issue is that you are making yourself angry, nothing else. It is simple. You can't forgive someone or yourself. You are holding a grudge or some unhealthy attachments. This is all in your mind and it is all influencing your day-to-day emotions and behaviours. Your ego is telling you that you can't accept what that person does. It is unforgivable. I would ask, really? Is that really true? It's in the past and you can't change it, and still, you are making yourself bothered about it? How is that helping you? There is a lot of regret and negative force within. Can you feel it? You are digging a deeper hole for yourself every day by using this language and keeping yourself in a cycle of anger, frustration, and hate that doesn't serve you and can make you ill.

Words such as *hate, can't, terrible,* or *horrible* evoke emotions in our emotional bodies and you already know the process—you release chemicals into your body and then you are in a cycle of negative thoughts and even stronger hateful words. You find yourself anxious and feeling stuck because your focus is fully on the negative aspects of this event or this person. You are totally disregarding any good in the bad situation or any learning opportunity in the negative events. Everything bad happens for a really good reason. Instead, you create a tunnel vision and you only see this negative as true. All positive aspects of this event have disappeared because your positive language around it has disappeared.

You can take yourself out of this event and negative feelings. You can ask yourself what was actually good about this event—what did you learn from it? Did you become stronger, smarter, more careful, or more experienced? Maybe you had to push harder to achieve more and you feel worthy and maybe a little proud of yourself because you overcame the challenge. You are on the other side stronger than ever. Maybe you had to move or you met someone because of this circumstance. Maybe you made some decisions you wouldn't have before, maybe you grew, or maybe you undertook some personal or professional development. I am sure you can find the positive side of each circumstance, because we know there is light in the dark and dark in the light.

Now, when you realise that the event or circumstance wasn't that horrible, you can use better words and shift your language around it. For example, it was a learning experience. Sounds better, right? How does it feel? How do you feel? Lighter? In peace? Free?

That's true. You will be able to exchange words for much lighter expressions and so influence your brain from negative to more optimistic. You will be able to change your outlook on life by changing your day-to-day language. Instead of *hate*, say *not my preference*. Instead of *horrible*, say it was a *learning experience* or maybe it *wasn't comfortable*.

There is another part of the language we are using in so-called self-talk. A lot of people say "I should," "I have to," or "I need to." Those words create a lot of internal pressure and sometimes even anxiety. Think about that and consider something you always say to yourself. Maybe you say, "I *should* go to the gym," or "I *should* tell them something." Now, try to say, instead, "I *will* go to the gym," or "I *will* tell them something." Does that feel lighter? It feels like a big release.

So, don't create extra pressure and anxiety within yourself by using the wrong language. Start to reprogram your mind with words that serve you. I'm sure that, if something you see today as *horrible* or the *worst that can happen to you*, you will call it a *learning experience* or *necessary for your growth* in the future. You will realise that these so-called bad times make you better, stronger, more resilient, and more successful.

Chapter 9

Stress and Pressure

WHAT IS STRESS AND WHAT DO WE DO TO COPE?

Stress and pressure are impediments to happiness, authenticity, and success. Stress and pressure might be seen as forces that push you out of alignment with your true self and hinder your ability to perform at your best.

Scientifically, stress is a physiological response that occurs when you perceive a threat or challenge. When faced with stressors, the body releases stress hormones such as cortisol and adrenaline, preparing it for fight or flight. While this response is essential for survival in immediate danger, chronic stress can have detrimental effects on physical and mental health.

Pressure, on the other hand, often refers to external expectations or demands placed on us, such as deadlines, performance targets, or societal norms. While pressure can motivate you to excel, excessive pressure can lead to anxiety, burnout, and decreased performance.

Stress can be addressed through techniques aimed at cultivating resilience, self-awareness, and inner peace. This involves practices rooted in psychology, neuroscience, and mindfulness to help you manage stress effectively and thrive in both your personal and professional lives.

Addressing stress and pressure involves a holistic approach centred around cultivating resilience, self-awareness, and inner peace. Let's have a look at what I mean by that. Let's take resilience. Resilience refers to the ability to bounce back from adversity and cope with life's challenges. I emphasise the importance of building resilience through strategies in this book; for example, reframing setbacks as opportunities for growth, developing problem-solving skills, fostering social support networks and relationships, and practising meditation, breathing, or other self-care routines.

Another amazing strategy that has helped me and my clients is to become more conscious at each moment and **self-aware**. Learn how to bring consciousness into the day. Why is that important? You'll gain access to wisdom at each moment of your day-to-day, and you will then become more intelligent and able to use a higher state and bigger capacity of your brain, not only using information and data you gain throughout your life by learning with the left brain but also being able to use the right brain more often. Self-awareness involves understanding one's thoughts, emotions, and behaviours.

Your approach could include techniques for increasing self-awareness, such as mindfulness, journalling, reflection exercises, meditation, and feedback. I have shared some of these techniques throughout this book, and the exercises you have completed focus on consistently increasing awareness.

Another great strategy is building **inner peace**, which entails developing a state of tranquillity and harmony within oneself despite external circumstances. What I do, and what I practise with my clients, is mindfulness meditation, gratitude exercises, visualisation techniques, and breathing techniques.

Drawing from principles of psychology, we use cognitive behavioural techniques, positive psychology interventions, and emotional regulation strategies. These approaches help my clients reframe negative thinking patterns, build resilience, and cultivate a more optimistic outlook on life.

Another approach we are using is incorporating neuroscience principles into stress management. We educate people about the brain's stress response system and how practices like mindfulness meditation can modulate the neural pathways associated with stress and resilience. Understanding the neuroscience behind stress will empower you, and we mentioned this in the first few chapters about the brain, how your brain works, and the amygdala, which we operate from most of the time. I gave you a few insights into this because I believe the more we understand it, the better we can manage it.

The number one stress management tool, and I believe the simplest to practise, is mindfulness. It involves paying attention to the present moment with openness, curiosity, and acceptance with no judgement and no preferences. You can use mindfulness meditation, body exercise, or mindful breathing techniques. I will share some of those at the end of this book. These practices help to develop greater emotional regulation, enhance your ability to cope with stress, and improve overall wellbeing.

Stress management is another one of those huge areas. I have found over the years that one of the most challenging and difficult things my clients are dealing with is stress; and in the world, stress kills.

All stress, it's important to know, is not created equal. Stress is not always negative, and this is something that we need to be able to see.

Some stress is normal; it's even desirable and healthy. When stress is managed, it can provide a competitive edge, for example, in performance-related activities such as athletics, public speaking, acting, and leadership. When stress is overwhelming or constant, however, heart disease, obesity, asthma, ulcers, and allergies can result.

Techniques for dealing with stress and pressure

Constant stress, whether from a traffic-choked daily commute, unhappy marriage, or heavy workload, can have real physical effects on the body. It has been linked to a wide range of health issues, including mood, sleep, and appetite problems, and yes, even heart disease.

We were born to be exposed to only short-term stress, and there is just a short switch on fight-or-flight mode and only one fast injection of cortisol. Mental stress activates your sympathetic nervous system, sending your body into fight-or-flight mode. During this reaction, stress hormones trigger physical symptoms such as a faster heartbeat, quicker breathing, and constricted blood vessels. Our response is shallow breathing or very fast breathing, which sends signals back to our body so the body has an even bigger stress response. This is how we create a cycle of never-ending or long-term stress. The quickest way to avoid this is to relearn our breathing response and utilise it to shift from stress mode to ease. That's why practising breathing techniques daily is beneficial; it helps your body establish a new breathing pattern. When you get stressed, it is going to use your newly learnt breathing pattern and not the stress-triggered shallow and fast breathing rhythm. Deep breathing exercises help activate your parasympathetic nervous system, which controls the relaxation response.

Deep breathing exercises include diaphragmatic breathing, abdominal breathing, and belly breathing, which are calming and have a releasing effect.

The goal of deep breathing is to focus your awareness on your breath, making it slower and deeper. When you breathe in deeply through your nose, your lungs fully expand and your belly rises. Make the exhale longer and slower and maybe even pause at the end before you take the next inhale. This helps slow your heart rate, allowing you to feel at peace. This is also when you are focused and fully aware of your breath, so you are practising mindfulness and awareness at the same time.

Today in the modern world, we are under constant stress. We have high cortisol all day long. That is a major problem, because our body is not naturally created for this amount of constant cortisol increase and this can cause various physical issues and problems.

We need to learn how to deal with stress and manage unhealthy habits. These five simple tips can help you do just that:

Stay positive. Laughter lowers levels of stress hormones, reduces inflammation in the arteries, and increases "good" HDL cholesterol.

Meditate. This practice of inward-focused thought and deep breathing reduces heart disease risk factors such as high blood pressure. Meditation's close relatives yoga and prayer can also relax the mind and body.

Exercise. Every time you are physically active, whether you take a walk or play tennis, your body releases mood-boosting chemicals called endorphins. Exercising not only helps you de-stress, but it also protects against heart disease by lowering your blood pressure, strengthening your heart muscle, and helping you maintain a healthy weight.

Unplug is my favourite to begin with. It's impossible to escape stress when it follows you everywhere. Cut the cord. Turn off your phone or leave it at home and go for a walk. Avoid emails and TV news. Take time each day, even if it's for just ten or fifteen minutes, to escape from the digital and commercial world.

Find ways to de-stress. Simple things, like a warm bath, listening to music, or spending time on a favourite hobby, can give you a much-needed break from the stressors in your life. I sing in the car or dance during the day for a few minutes between my meetings. All I do is change and shift my energy and inner feelings. Change your state by breaking the patterns of sitting, calling, or email reading.

We talk a lot about **leadership.** One of the major skills to have is to be able to relieve stress and also help your team members to do the same. There is nothing worse than a team operating from high stress levels.

After this chapter, do you know how to help yourself or others in your team?

There are a lot of techniques that can help with stress. One of the concepts we use is to understand that your thoughts, emotions, and actions are closely connected. The way you think and feel about something can affect what you do. If you are under stress at work, you might see situations differently and, based on that, make choices and decisions you wouldn't ordinarily make. We teach leaders and team members how those behavioural and thinking patterns can be changed.

The most important is to understand and be aware that psychological or mental issues or a lot of stress are partly based on:

- negative or unresourceful ways of thinking
- learnt patterns of unhelpful behaviour and habits
- unhelpful coping mechanisms and inability to relieve their symptoms.

Negative or inaccurate perceptions or thoughts contribute to emotional distress, and this can lead to unhelpful behaviours. We already talked about our brain and our thinking, and now we are in the next step—our behaviours. We mentioned reframing, which can be one of your leadership tools to help your team think differently and then reduce stress.

A little recap on how to address these limiting patterns and re-work them:

- Build awareness and understanding
- Foster self-assessment, such as profiling and strengths/gaps analysis
- Learn how to overcome challenges and fears
- Self-coaching and coaching with insights training
- Basic power questions and frameworks leading towards positive thinking
- Reframing

- Breathing techniques
- Meditation
- Healthy lifestyle
- Mindfulness

The cycle of thoughts and behaviours

Here's a closer look at how thoughts and emotions can influence behaviour in a positive or negative way.

Inaccurate or negative perceptions or thoughts contribute to emotional distress and mental health concerns. These thoughts and the resulting distress sometimes lead to unhelpful or harmful behaviours. Eventually, these thoughts and resulting behaviours can become a pattern that repeats itself. And now, you are running your life on autopilot.

Learning how to address and change these patterns can help you deal with problems as they arise, which can help reduce future distress. That's why coaching and mentoring are so important to me. I can tell I am a pretty aware and awake person, but still, so many times it's great to have someone who can call me on my limits and challenge me so I develop further and deeper.

Reworking patterns often involves the following:

- Recognising how inaccurate our thinking can be and how that can worsen problems
- Learning new problem-solving skills
- Gaining confidence
- Better understanding and appreciating your self-worth
- Learning how to face fears and challenges
- Using roleplay and calming techniques when faced with potentially challenging situations

The goal of these techniques is to replace unhelpful or self-defeating thoughts with more encouraging and realistic ones.

For example, "I'll never have a lasting relationship" might become "None of my previous relationships have lasted very long. Reconsidering what I really need from a partner could help me find someone I'll be compatible with long-term."

We are here to learn more about our conditioning and where it is all coming from. A great example came from the psychologist Maslow and his hierarchy of needs, later developed by Tony Robbins into the "core needs" concept. I love this concept, so I'll give you a little bit of an overview. It will show you how naturally we are conditioned and what needs we need to fulfil first. If we lack fulfilment of any of those needs, our behaviours adjust and change. That's why it is so important to understand all our behaviours, drivers, and motivators to act appropriately.

Some of the techniques that can help us to change our behaviours and actions:

Self-talk. Take note of what you tell yourself about a certain situation or experience and challenge yourself to replace negative or critical self-talk with compassionate, constructive self-talk.

Cognitive restructuring. This involves looking at any cognitive distortions affecting your thoughts—such as black-and-white thinking, jumping to conclusions, or catastrophising—and beginning to unravel them. Challenge your thinking. Even 1+1 is not always 2.

Thought recording. In this technique, you'll record thoughts and feelings experienced during a specific situation, then come up with unbiased evidence supporting your negative belief and evidence against it. You'll use this evidence to develop a more realistic thought.

Positive activities. Scheduling a rewarding activity each day can help. Some examples might be buying yourself fresh flowers or fruit, watching your favourite movie, or having a picnic lunch at the park.

Situation exposure. *I would suggest doing this under guidance.* This involves listing situations or things that cause distress in order of the level of distress they cause and slowly exposing yourself to these things until they lead to fewer negative feelings. Systematic desensitisation is a similar technique where you'll learn relaxation techniques to help you cope with your feelings in a difficult situation.

In terms of coaching a team that is dealing with stress, there are a variety of techniques that I can suggest, and many of you are probably familiar with some of these. Some of these techniques will resonate with you and some will not, so it's especially important here to know yourself or your team members. Examples we use are breathing techniques, progressive relaxation, mediation, and visualisation.

Core needs—our internal drivers

This concept was developed by Tony Robbins, and it came from Maslow's hierarchy of needs. I won't take long with this. I'll share the part that helped me to understand my relationships and myself the most so you can see deeper within yourself and see why you are not feeling fulfilled or satisfied.

Remember, it is not because of money, time, or circumstances. It is because of the *emotion* surrounding time, money, or circumstance. It is because of your internal sense of misaligned or unfulfilled core needs.

Let's have a look at what those needs are. In short, there is a need for certainty, uncertainty, significance, connection, growth, and contributions. We have a combination of all of them, so we need to fulfil them all at different levels. So, for example, my high core needs are variety and uncertainty, but at the same time, I need some level of certainty and safety. It is a different level or percentage of those we need based on our core personality and preferred needs. Think about yourself. What are your core needs?

I would suggest doing a short exercise to discover your core needs so you find out which one is the most important for you personally. But first read about all the needs to understand them better.

The need for certainty

Also known as the need for comfort, safety, security, or control.

This is the need to feel safe and in control to know what's coming next so we can feel secure. It's the need for basic comfort, the need to avoid pain and stress, but also to create pleasure by warding off anxiety and worry.

Our need for certainty is a survival mechanism. It affects how much risk we are willing to take in our lives, jobs, investments, and relationships. The more certainty we seek, the fewer risks we take. We all need certainty in our lives; how we get that certainty, whether through controlling others or through believing in ourselves, determines the quality of our lives.

The more we think our environment must change for us to feel certain, the less quality of life we have. The more we take responsibility for our own sense of certainty, the greater our feelings of self-worth and thus the better we feel about our lives.

What did I do to feel safe in times of uncertainty? During the pandemic and when relocating to a new country to start my business without a network, I faced immense uncertainty. To create a sense of stability, I focused on activities that provided certainty and comfort. Running became my anchor; I excelled at it and knew exactly how to incorporate it into my daily routine. Exercise, with its predictable outcomes, also became a staple. Cooking, a creative outlet I thoroughly enjoyed, brought me a sense of control amidst chaos.

One of the most reassuring routines I established was visiting the same coffee shop, where I met familiar faces for uplifting conversations. These interactions provided a sense of community and familiarity in an otherwise unfamiliar environment. By embracing these activities that offered certainty and comfort, I navigated through uncertain times with resilience and determination.

The need for variety

Also known as the need for uncertainty, adventure, or challenge.

The flip side of certainty is uncertainty, also known as variety. So, while we need some level of certainty to function, we also need some level of variety to spice things up.

If things are too predictable for too long, we get bored, so we look for adventure or challenge to feel variety. How we do this tells us a lot about the quality of our lives.

If things are cruising along, for example, in a relationship, and we're "settled", do we stir things up by picking a fight, or do we stir things up by doing something spontaneous and romantic?

Both create variety, but the first response is going to create a lower quality of life, and the second choice can improve our quality of life immensely. One response is functional and resourceful. One response is unresourceful.

To balance the need for variety amidst my quest for certainty, I consciously incorporated diverse activities into my daily life. Each day, I explored new places, driving to different areas to acquaint myself with the surroundings. Walking my dogs on various beaches added spontaneity and discovery to my routine. On weekends, I ventured to distant locales for activities like swimming and learning to surf, fostering a sense of adventure and exploration.

The monotony of solitary computer work in my home office prompted me to seek social interaction. Instead of isolated lunches, I opted for outdoor lunches in parks, engaging with strangers and fostering new connections. These varied experiences not only enriched my daily life but also provided a healthy balance between familiarity and novelty, fulfilling both my need for certainty and my need for variety. This way I was able to keep myself balanced and happy.

The need for significance

Also known as the need for respect or appreciation.

This one is interesting. The need for significance can be met or driven through our egos, which can be tiresome and grating on others.

The need for significance means that you are constantly striving to feel important, special, unique, or worthy. Having goals you would like to achieve, a list of incredible skills you want to develop, and a wealth status you would like to attain provides you with significance and a sense of accomplishment.

You naturally gain significance when, in comparison to others, you reach a stage where you feel more important and worthy. You can feel more significant by achieving something, by building something, by learning something, or even by tearing other people down. They are all legitimate ways to fulfil the need for significance.

Meeting this need can be done through providing service to others and giving. It can be met through doing something that you are proud of, through blaming someone, through yelling and fits of anger ….

There are lots of ways to meet this need, some harmful and some helpful. If you blame others for your mess, you're meeting your need for significance. If you take responsibility for the mess, you're meeting your need for significance.

Both accomplish meeting the need, it's just one way is unresourceful and one way is resourceful. One way will mess you up more. One way will propel you forward. Either way, the need is being met.

To fulfill my need for significance, I consistently created opportunities to make a meaningful impact. For instance, I regularly offered scholarships or provided free coaching to individuals in need. Volunteering became a significant part of my life during my initial years in Australia, allowing me to contribute to my community and beyond. These acts not only satisfied my desire for significance but also enriched my journey by positively impacting the lives of others. Volunteering or helping people in need became a normal part of my life that not only provides a feeling of self-respect but also fulfils a need for contribution, growth, love and connection.

The need for connection

Also known as the need for love.

We all need to feel connected in some way. Love and connection are the oxygen of life.

The need for connection means that you are constantly striving to build strong social bonds and relationships with other people. This is the main reason we get married, attend church gatherings, spend time in nature, gather at clubs, and why some people choose to join gangs. It's all because of a need to feel connected to other people in some way.

We may get this need met through a relationship, meditation, exercise, writing a book, having a coffee with a friend or even a combination of these.

And we could get it through taking drugs, smoking, drinking, or arguing.

One way or another, we *will* get this need met, and as with the other needs, it will either be in a way that is resourceful or unresourceful.

For those who dare to venture, these last two needs will determine your level of happiness and fulfilment in your life.

The need for growth

The need for growth means that you are constantly striving to learn new skills, to gather knowledge, and to grow as a person. You have this picture of yourself in the future, of how you desire to be. And your need for growth is pushing you to reach for that ideal self.

If a relationship is not growing, if a business is not growing, if you're not growing, it doesn't matter how much money you have in the bank, how many friends you have, or how many people love you, you're not going to experience real fulfilment.

And the reason we grow is so we have something of value to give.

When the need for growth is at its highest, you are continuously striving to grow emotionally, spiritually, physically, financially, and intellectually. As a result, you might learn a new skill, you might choose to read books, you might take a class or apply to university, and so on.

Growth is a very important aspect of life. If you are not growing, then you are making no real progress in life. However, growth isn't necessarily about learning a new skill or about reading a book. It's more about the time you put into yourself—reflection, and about how mindful you are of the consequences of your daily decisions, choices, and actions.

If we grow, we feel good about ourselves, our self-worth goes up, our confidence builds, we feel more certainty and can experience more variety, and we feel significant.

If you're not green and growing, you're ripe and rotting.

Without growth, life stagnates, and we feel like we are shrinking, like something is lacking, and we experience the feelings of being stuck in a rut with a sense of dissatisfaction.

If you're not feeling that great about yourself, it could be because you have been avoiding doing the very things that could lead to learning and growth.

The need for contribution

This final need is another pathway to happiness and fulfilment. When we get to give to others beyond ourselves, it seems to cause our own problems to fade! The secret of living is giving.

The need for contribution means that you are living out your life's purpose and providing value to others that goes beyond your own needs, desires, and wants. You are essentially living for a higher purpose, for something greater than yourself that can potentially last a lifetime and beyond.

Exercise—core needs discovery:

Ask yourself, if you could only choose one of each of the pairs below, which would it be:

- Certainty or uncertainty?
- Safety or variety?
- Security or adventure?
- Comfort or challenge?
- Significance or connection?

Now, pair up your responses and ask the same question with those pairs. Repeat the process until you have one core need left. That is your highest core need to focus on for fulfilment. Now, to gain clarity, think about the last major decision you made in your life. Ask yourself: "How did I make that decision? What factors did I consider?" This will give you more clarity about the core need that plays a significant role in your decision-making process.

Chapter 10

Practical Rules for a Fulfilled Life

Have you ever wondered what fulfilment is? How does it feel when you are living a fulfilled life?

Well, I have asked those questions many times.

Almost a decade ago, I moved to Western Australia and lived in a place I hated. I never wanted to move there, but I managed, and I tried to find my place. I learnt about a culture that was foreign to me and thought I would try to fit in. As I mentioned before, that wasn't a great idea. I tried so hard to be the same as everyone, to be accepted, to feel like I belonged and was good enough. I was hungry for deeper connections, for a real friend, for the feeling of familiarity and acceptance that you have with old friends from your childhood. I am sure you know that feeling when you can be yourself, just being you. When no-one judges you or compares you.

While searching for acceptance and connections, I felt more and more deprived of connections and moved further and further from my authentic self. I stopped understanding myself and wasn't sure what I wanted anymore. It not only felt like I was stuck, but I felt more and more like giving up. I was exhausted, tired, and burnt out because all day long, my major focus was on business and work. I didn't have too much free time because I wasn't able to even think about how I wanted to spend it. Mental exhaustion feels insane. It creates tunnel vision, a strong focus on one and only small thing because the capacity of the brain and creativity is shrinking from the constant stress of inner fighting with reality and the environment. Inner fighting means resistance—constant resistance.

There was no piece of acceptance or self-esteem left. *Lost* is the only word that describes it. I lost passion, excitement, and big-picture thinking. I lived in the one small place inside that hated and resented everything because of the circumstances I wasn't able to accept.

One day, I woke up and saw my miserable mood from far away. It felt like I was observing myself from above, as if I were watching someone else's life unfold. I saw myself from a helicopter view, detached from the weight I had been carrying. At that moment, I realised I didn't like who I had become. I had spent so much energy trying to be someone else—someone driven by comparison and chasing approval—and constantly felt that I was missing something. I had been lost in the pursuit of fitting in rather than stepping into who I truly wanted to be.

That day was a turning point. I didn't just decide to change—I decided to **become** the version of myself I admired. I began asking, *Who do I want to be today? How does that version of me think, act, and show up? How do I show up for myself and for others?*

I understood that my identity wasn't something fixed—it was fluid, shaped by the choices I made each day. And from that identity, aligned actions naturally followed. When I stepped into the identity of someone grounded, joyful, and intentional, my decisions reflected that version of me. Those decisions started creating new results in my life.

I began the work of healing. I dove into removing old subconscious blockages and limiting beliefs using the techniques I now share with my clients. It wasn't overnight, but within a week of deeply committing to the process, I felt shifts. I danced, I laughed, and I reconnected with the lightness of life.

I stopped seeing life as something to be achieved and started living it as a gift. Instead of focusing on fitting in, I stood out. I stopped wondering how others perceived me, and for the first time, I let that be irrelevant. I aligned with what felt right—day by day, moment by moment. I followed what resonated deeply within me.

I began speaking my truth. This was more than words; it was an energetic shift. I noticed a shift around my throat chakra—the energy centre associated with communication, self-expression, and speaking one's truth.

For those unfamiliar, the **throat chakra** is part of the body's energy system. It sits at the base of the throat and governs our ability to express ourselves honestly and clearly. When this chakra is balanced, we can speak our minds confidently, articulate our feelings, and communicate with authenticity. However, when blocked, we may feel unheard, afraid to express our ideas, or hesitant to share our true selves.

At that time, I realised my throat chakra had been blocked for a long while. I struggled to say what I truly felt and often avoided confrontation, swallowing my words to keep the peace. But as I healed, I felt the energy move. I began to communicate more clearly and confidently. It became easier to express who I was and what I needed.

Suddenly, I felt understood. The sense of isolation I once carried—feeling like no one could hear or see me—slowly faded away. The more I spoke from my heart, the more I connected deeply with those around me.

From that time onward, everything changed. I started crossing paths with extraordinary, values-aligned people—people on their own journeys of spiritual growth, people seeking deeper meaning, connection, and understanding. I no longer chased these connections. They came naturally because I was embodying the identity of someone who attracted them.

Every day began to feel like a miracle. Conversations felt like gifts. Every session I had with my clients became more than a service—it felt like a full-body, heart-centred experience. The energy I carried transformed the spaces I entered. The more I aligned, the more magic I created. I felt like I was truly living for the first time.

Wealth and external achievements became a byproduct, not the goal. Success no longer defined me; it simply reflected the alignment I had cultivated. What became primary was the joy I felt, the love I poured into my work, and the peace that followed me each day.

I started to notice something beautiful—every time someone stepped into a room I occupied, the collective energy shifted. The higher frequency I held naturally elevated those around me. It's what continues to fulfil me—helping others step into their higher selves, guiding them to realise that life isn't meant to be lived in survival mode.

Life is a gift. We can choose to live it with gratitude and passion or in desperation and fear. The choice is always ours.

I've learned that the results we seek don't come from endlessly chasing outcomes. They come from becoming the person who naturally creates those results. It starts with identity—Who do I want to be today? Aligned action flows from that place, and those actions shape the reality we experience.

And this brings me to the first rule of a fulfilled life: decision.

The decision to choose **who you are becoming**—every single day.

1. Make the decision

When you try to stop an addiction, drinking alcohol, or smoking cigarettes, it is not going to change or be sustainable without shifting beliefs about yourself and your relationship with alcohol or cigarettes. Making a decision is indeed the cornerstone of creating lasting change in life. When it comes to overcoming addictions like alcohol or smoking, the process often involves more than just willpower or short-term abstinence. Without a genuine and deep-seated decision to change, you may find yourself slipping back into old habits despite your initial efforts to quit.

The key lies in the depth of the decision-making process. It's not merely about saying, "I want to quit," but rather about fully committing to that decision on a profound level. This entails examining your beliefs and motivations surrounding the addiction. Without addressing these underlying beliefs and making a conscious shift in mindset, the desire to quit may remain superficial and fleeting.

For example, someone struggling with alcohol addiction may have deeply ingrained beliefs about alcohol's role in coping with stress or social situations. So many times, my clients expressed or said, "I am so tired and exhausted at the end of the day that the only thing I look forward to is to sit down and have a glass of wine or whisky to release."

Without challenging and reshaping these beliefs, simply abstaining from alcohol may feel like deprivation rather than liberation. Thus, without a genuine shift in mindset and a firm decision to break free from the addiction and autopilot, the cycle of relapse may continue. One day, you realise that this habit of having a release and a "feel-good" drink after work has continued for the past ten years, and you may be addicted.

In essence, making the decision to change is not just about the action itself but about transforming one's internal landscape. It involves confronting limiting beliefs, redefining priorities, reframing, committing to a new way of living, and creating a connection with a clear internal reward system. By doing so, you can pave the way for sustainable and fulfilling change in your life, and you can apply this approach to any addictions. Life without addiction is freedom.

Let's move on to the second rule.

2. Self-study

Understand the times and states in which you operate the best. What do you need as a routine to feel recharged daily? What do you need to eat to feel healthy and inspired? What do you need to do or practise to gain control over your energetic body?

Self-study is a fundamental principle that underpins personal growth and success. From my perspective at the Mentoring Effect, it's about cultivating a deep understanding of oneself to optimise performance, emotions, energy, and wellbeing.

Understanding the times when you operate at your best is crucial. Self-study encompasses a comprehensive examination of oneself, including understanding the times and states when you operate at your best. This involves recognising not only the hours of the day but also the conditions and circumstances that optimise your performance. For me, this means identifying the environments, activities, and mindsets that enable me to tap into my fullest potential. What are your environments, activities, or mindsets for greater performance and fulfilment?

Moreover, self-study involves establishing routines that facilitate daily recharge. This includes identifying practices that rejuvenate the mind, body, and soul. For instance, incorporating regular exercise, meditation, journalling, or time spent in nature can help replenish energy reserves and maintain overall wellbeing. By prioritising these activities as part of your daily routine, you can ensure sustained vitality and resilience. As we know, emotional and cognitive states have a direct impact on your cells. Our body creates around 800,000 new cells daily. When we create a healthy environment with positive emotions and mindset, we can heal or re-create new healthy cells. If we destroy our inner environment with negative thoughts, pessimistic emotions, or fears, the body produces chemicals so we have an unhealthy environment that creates more damaged cells and can therefore result in illness.

In terms of nutrition, self-study entails understanding how different foods impact your physical and mental health. This involves experimenting and creating your own way of eating and enjoying food. For me, this means creating a mindset that food is medicine. I am always reminding myself that my body is like a car. I have to be careful not to put petrol in my diesel car. Just as using the wrong type of fuel in a car can lead to malfunction or damage, consuming the wrong foods or neglecting self-care practices can have negative consequences for your health. By listening to my body's signals and honouring its nutritional needs, I can cultivate a diet that nourishes and inspires me.

Furthermore, self-study extends to gaining control over your energetic body. This involves working with coaches or mentors and exploring practices such as breathwork, mindfulness, and energy healing modalities to cultivate greater awareness and mastery over your energetic state. By incorporating these practices into your daily routine, you will be able to enhance your ability to regulate your energy levels, manage stress, and cultivate inner balance.

Self-study is a journey of self-discovery and self-care. It requires a commitment to exploring and understanding oneself on physical, mental, emotional, and energetic levels. By investing in self-study, you unlock your full potential, optimise your wellbeing, and live a life aligned with your deepest values and aspirations.

3. Take a break

Taking a step back from day-to-day will help you to widen your vision and stop being so narrow-minded. It helps you to see everything from a bigger perspective. If you can't solve the problem or don't know how to move forward, stepping back and taking a break will help you to use the right brain to find logical answers instead of relying only on the left, factual brain.

Taking a break is more than just a pause in your daily routine; it's a deliberate act of self-care and introspection that can profoundly impact your overall emotional state and perspective on life. In the fast-paced world we live in, it's easy to get caught up in the hustle of day-to-day activities, often leading to a narrow-minded focus on immediate tasks and challenges we see in front of us right now. However, by intentionally stepping back and allowing yourself the space to rest and recharge, you create an opportunity to widen your vision and gain a broader perspective. If you are too close to the problem, you can't see the solution—you can't see the forest for the trees.

When you take a break, whether it's a short walk in nature, a meditation session, or a weekend getaway, you allow your mind to disengage from the minutiae of daily life and tap into the creative and intuitive capabilities of your right brain. Even small things, like changing activities for a few minutes, can help, and things such as stopping trying to solve unsolvable problems and taking a really deep breath so you pause. Look around and do a new activity for the next ten minutes. This shift in focus enables you to see problems and challenges from a fresh angle, often revealing insights and solutions that may have eluded you in your narrow-minded state. Or sometimes, you realise there is no actual problem.

Moreover, taking a break fosters mental clarity and emotional resilience. It allows you to approach challenges with a renewed sense of energy and purpose. By temporarily stepping away from your responsibilities, you create space for reflection, self-discovery, and personal growth. In this way, taking breaks becomes not only a means of relaxation but also a powerful tool for problem-solving and decision-making.

Regular breaks are essential for maintaining balance and preventing burnout. In today's hyper-connected world, where technology blurs the boundaries between work and personal life, it's more important than ever to prioritise downtime and disconnect from the constant barrage of stimuli. By setting boundaries and carving out time for rest and rejuvenation, you safeguard your mental and physical wellbeing, ensuring that you can show up at your best in all areas of life.

In fact, taking a break is not a luxury but a necessity for living a fulfilled life. It allows you to recharge your batteries, gain perspective, and approach challenges with clarity and creativity.

4. Vision and goals

Having vision and goals without a strong attachment is essential. However, it's equally important to maintain a mindset of non-attachment. From my perspective, this principle emphasises the importance of setting intentions and working towards goals while remaining flexible and open to unforeseen opportunities, changes, and outcomes.

Having a vision provides a sense of direction and purpose, guiding your actions and decisions towards a desired future. Setting goals allows you to break down your vision into actionable steps and milestones, providing a roadmap for progress. However, attaching too strongly to specific outcomes can lead to rigidity and tunnel vision that misses out on bigger opportunities and creates disappointment especially when things don't unfold exactly as planned.

Embracing a mindset of non-attachment allows you to hold your vision and goals lightly, remaining open to the infinite possibilities that life may present. It means releasing the need for control and surrendering to the flow of life, trusting that the universe will guide us towards our highest good. Remember, life is happening for you.

Practising non-attachment doesn't mean abandoning your goals or vision. Rather, it means detaching from the outcome while remaining committed to the journey. It involves focusing on the process and enjoying the journey rather than fixating on the end result, allowing room for growth, adaptation, and serendipity along the way.

By practising non-attachment, you free yourself from the constraints of fear and expectation, opening yourself up to new opportunities and experiences that may align more closely with your true desires and aspirations. It fosters resilience, adaptability, and a deeper sense of inner peace, even in the face of uncertainty and change. Having a vision without a strong attachment is about finding the delicate balance between ambition and acceptance, determination and surrender. It's about embracing the journey with an open heart and mind, trusting that each step forward brings you closer to your highest potential, regardless of the specific outcomes you may encounter along the way.

5. Time

Time, as you perceive it, is not just a linear progression of moments but also deeply intertwined with your emotions and perceptions. From my perspective, recognising this connection allows for a more harmonious relationship with time.

Impatience often stems from a sense of urgency or the desire for immediate results. However, rushing through life can lead to stress, anxiety, exhaustion, burnout, and a lack of presence in the present moment. When you cultivate impatience, you may be on the way to creating shallow connections and not very fulfilled relationships or even lose some friends or business opportunities. Who wants to be around a person who is always in a rush or always busy? You don't want to be around impatient people, and I can tell you why. Most of the time, you will feel like you don't matter and you are not important around the impatient person because all that is important for this person is their goal or getting something out of the situation. If you are in a group of people who have a mindset of "I need to get it now," people won't like you. They will avoid you. And you will feel disconnected, lonely, and withdrawn. You won't succeed with this mindset and also you will create a lot of anxiety by cultivating impatience as a state of being.

Celebrating the mindset that everything unfolds in its own time allows for a sense of calm and trust in the process.

Setting goals and milestones is important for progress, but it's equally crucial to maintain flexibility and adaptability in your timelines. While having a clear timeframe can provide structure and motivation, becoming too fixated on deadlines can lead to unnecessary pressure and frustration.

Making peace with time involves acknowledging that everyone operates on the same 24-hour clock. It's not about having more or less time but rather about how you choose to use it. By prioritising what truly matters and focusing on the present moment, you make the most of your time and create a sense of fulfilment and satisfaction. As a leader, the same rule applies. Choose high-value activities, prioritise wisely, and focus on growing and improving your team members rather than other less important activities. Leverage. Leverage as much as you can. Delegate as much as you can.

Don't forget to recognise that growth and achievement often take time, so you should reduce the pressure to rush and allow for more gradual and sustainable progress. Trusting in the divine timing of events and embracing patience leads to greater peace of mind and a deeper appreciation for the journey. Not only that, but it leads to freedom and wealth.

Time is not something to be conquered or controlled but rather embraced and respected.

6. No regrets; no fears

This rule embodies a powerful principle for living a fulfilled life—embracing a mindset free from the burdens of regret and fear. From my perspective, it's about taking ownership of your decisions and actions and moving forward with confidence and conviction.

Regret and fear are two emotions that can weigh heavily on the human spirit, hindering personal growth and fulfilment. Regret often stems from dwelling on past mistakes or missed opportunities, while fear can paralyse you from taking risks and pursuing your dreams. I realised the importance of the "no regrets" rule after a client's session. I was sitting with my client, who wanted to separate from her partner but kept getting stuck on regrets. She was paralysed by fear of the future and a lack of money, and at the same time, she fed her fear with the question "What if I regret it?" So I asked her if she regretted anything in her life. Her answer was "everything". That was a big surprise to me, and I explained that this had been her way of living her life for fifty-two years.

I told her, "You are living in an emotion of regret. That doesn't sound like fun."

She asked me, "What do you mean? Don't you regret anything?"

I said, "No, I truly don't regret anything in my life."

We started a big session on unlocking the emotional home of scarcity, fear, and regret so she could move on. It's really hard to make any decision for a person who lives in a regretful state. I imagine that she already knew she would regret every decision she made because that was how she had lived her life until then. But we broke the pattern of these emotions that didn't serve her. We freed her from all her fears and regrets and she was free to make a decision for herself to stay or separate from her partner. She made her decision. She separated. She is the happiest person in the world right now, living her fulfilled life and improving her self-esteem by making decisions for herself more often without doubts and regrets.

By committing to a life free from regret and fear, you open yourself up to endless possibilities and opportunities for growth.

Making decisions with intention and conviction is key to living with no regrets. It's about trusting your instincts, following your heart, and accepting that every choice you make contributes to your personal journey and growth. Even if a decision doesn't yield the desired outcome, reframing it as a learning experience rather than a failure will help mitigate feelings of regret.

Confronting and overcoming fears is essential for personal empowerment, self-esteem, and fulfilment. Rather than allowing fear to dictate your actions, you choose to confront it head-on, stepping outside of your comfort zone and embracing new challenges with courage and resilience. By reframing fear as an opportunity for growth and expansion, you break free from its grip and pursue your dreams with confidence and determination.

Living without regrets, doubts, and fears doesn't mean ignoring the lessons of the past or the potential risks of the future. Instead, it's about adopting a mindset of mindfulness and presence, focusing on the here and now. Embracing each moment as it comes. By letting go of the past and releasing anxiety about the future, you will fully immerse yourself in the present moment and live life to the fullest.

Rule number six encourages you to be bold, take risks, and embrace the unknown with open arms.

7. Watch your thoughts

This rule underscores the profound influence that your thoughts have on your life and experiences. It emphasises the importance of mindfulness and self-awareness in shaping your reality.

Your thoughts serve as the directors of your life, guiding your perceptions, emotions, energy, and actions. What you think ultimately shapes the reality you experience, influencing how you interpret events, interact with others, and navigate the world around you. It's crucial to pay attention to the quality and content of your thoughts. When you think about the context and content of your life, you can't choose the content at each moment, but you can change or choose the context. So, for example, you can look at dying from the perspective of fear, regrets, and sadness, or you can see death as a celebration of life and being grateful for what you experienced and lived. You are not changing the content, which is death in this example, but you choose the context, your perception, and your thoughts.

The principle that "what you think, you become" highlights the power of your thoughts in creating your reality. When you focus on positive, empowering thoughts, you attract more positivity into your life and cultivate a mindset of abundance and possibility. Conversely, dwelling on negative, self-limiting thoughts hinders your progress and perpetuates feelings of doubt and limitation.

Your thoughts not only impact your internal landscape but also influence your external circumstances and material world. The energy you emit through your thoughts affects the vibrations you send out into the universe, attracting similar energies and experiences into your life. Therefore, it's essential to cultivate a mindset of positivity and abundance, consciously choosing thoughts that align with your goals and aspirations.

Being mindful of your thoughts involves monitoring your internal dialogue and challenging negative or self-defeating beliefs. Negative self-talk and harmful language, even if it's happening in your mind only and no-one is listening, can cause a lot of harm, unresourceful behaviours, and bad decisions. By cultivating a practice of self-awareness and introspection, you can identify thought patterns that no longer serve you and replace them with more empowering alternatives.

Rule number seven reminds you of the profound influence that your thoughts have on your life and experiences.

8. Perseverance and faith

When you cultivate faith, you align yourself with higher vibrations of energy and emotional states such as trust, hope, enthusiasm, and positivity. These elevated frequencies resonate with the universal laws of attraction and manifestation, drawing similar energies and experiences into your lives. As a leader, when you walk in this state in your work environment or business setting, you attract great talent and people who are committed, passionate, and take ownership.

At a quantum level, your thoughts and emotions emit energetic vibrations that interact with the quantum field around you. When you hold steadfast faith and belief in your goals and desires, you transmit powerful energetic signals that ripple out into the universe, influencing the fabric of reality.

This alignment with higher frequencies of energy and emotion creates a ripple effect that permeates every aspect of your being, from your thoughts and beliefs to your actions and experiences. It shifts your perception of the world around you, opening your eyes to new possibilities and opportunities that were previously unseen.

The energetic frequency of faith acts as a magnet, attracting people, circumstances, and resources that are in resonance with your desires and intentions. I am sure you've heard the quote from my favourite author, Napoleon Hill: "Whatever your mind can conceive and believe, it can achieve." This quote became the success and fulfilment guide for me and my clients.

As you maintain a state of faith and trust, you become the co-creator of your reality, actively shaping your experiences through the power of your thoughts and emotions.

The tangible changes that result from cultivating faith are often profound and far-reaching. They may manifest as synchronicities, serendipitous encounters, or unexpected blessings that align with your deepest desires and aspirations. These manifestations serve as tangible evidence of the transformative power of faith and its ability to create real change in the material world.

By aligning ourselves with the energy of faith and maintaining positive emotional states, you tap into the limitless potential of the universe to manifest your dreams into reality. Through the power of our thoughts, emotions, and beliefs, you become conscious co-creators of our destiny, shaping a life filled with purpose, abundance, and fulfilment.

Perseverance is more than just persistence; it's a mindset, a commitment, and a way of life. It's the unwavering determination to keep moving forward despite obstacles, setbacks, and challenges that may arise along the way. I see perseverance as a foundational principle for achieving success and fulfilment in both personal and professional life.

At its core, perseverance embodies resilience—the ability to bounce back from adversity stronger and more determined than ever. It's about facing challenges head-on, learning from failures, and using setbacks as opportunities for growth and self-improvement.

Perseverance is fuelled by passion and purpose. It's the driving force that propels you forward in pursuit of your goals and dreams, even when the path ahead is uncertain or difficult. And as you know, the path is not always easy. It's what keeps you going when others might give up, reminding you of the importance of staying true to your vision and values. That's why I see vision and goals as an important part of this. All the rules above are interconnected. Without vision, you might lose passion because you don't know where you are going, so there is nothing to persevere with.

Perseverance is also a source of inspiration and motivation for those around us. When others see us persevering in the face of adversity, it encourages them to do the same, creating a ripple effect of resilience and determination that uplifts and empowers the entire community. So, as a leader, you have the responsibility to cultivate this energy and state.

9. Passion and liveliness

Imagine walking into a room where people aren't expecting you—perhaps they've been talking about you. As you enter, you feel the weight of their piercing eyes on you, and you sense the disappointment in those who see you there. This scenario is the opposite of liveliness—it's a feeling of being unwelcome and disconnected.

Now, contrast that with walking into a room full of people gathered for your birthday party, and you had no idea they'd be there. Picture the energy in the room, the excitement, and the way everyone jumps up to greet you. Can you feel the difference?

In one scenario, there's a sense of heaviness and discomfort, while in the other, there's an explosion of joy and liveliness. It's a vivid illustration of how your surroundings and the energy of those around you can profoundly impact your experience of liveliness.

Passion and liveliness are the fuel that lights up your spirit and propels you forward in life. Passion and liveliness embody a vibrant energy and vitality that is contagious and inspiring to those around you.

Passion is the fire within you that drives you to pursue your dreams, follow your heart, and embrace life with enthusiasm and zest. It's the deep-seated love and excitement for what you do that fuels your creativity, determination, and resilience in the face of challenges.

Liveliness, on the other hand, is the vibrant energy that radiates from within you when you are fully present and engaged in the moment. It's the feeling of being fully alive, awake, and aware of the beauty and wonder of life unfolding around you. Liveliness is contagious, spreading joy, positivity, and inspiration to everyone you meet and everyone you spend time with.

Together, passion and liveliness create a positive outlook on life that transforms challenges into opportunities, obstacles into stepping stones, and setbacks into lessons for growth. They enable you to approach life with a "yes" mindset, embracing new experiences and opportunities with open arms rather than succumbing to fear or negativity.

Living with passion and liveliness means choosing optimism over pessimism, creativity over conformity, and joy over despair. It's about seeing possibilities where others see limitations, finding solutions where others see problems, and embracing life with a sense of wonder and curiosity.

If you set the intention and use this rule as a theme for your week or even just a day, the transformative power of this rule will change your life and your experience forever.

Now, a little clarification. Liveliness is a choice. You can choose to do things that put your energy down and make you feel terrible, or you can choose to do what you love, what makes you feel fulfilled and alive. It is a choice of your path. You can stay in desperation and think that things are horrible right now, or you can choose to bring a positive outlook and live through those challenges with the power of passion and liveliness.

10. Eat the frog

"Eat the frog" is a popular productivity concept popularised by Brian Tracy in his book of the same name. The idea behind "eating the frog" is to tackle your most challenging or important task first thing in the morning, rather than procrastinating or avoiding it. By completing your most difficult task early in the day, you set yourself up for a sense of accomplishment and momentum that can carry you through the rest of your tasks with greater efficiency and ease. In essence, it's about prioritising your time and energy on what matters most, rather than getting bogged down by smaller, less significant tasks.

"Eating the frog" is about confronting your biggest challenges head-on rather than procrastinating or avoiding them. It's about facing discomfort and uncertainty with courage and determination, knowing that by doing so, you're clearing the path for greater success and fulfilment.

11. What you want versus what you don't want

This rule highlights the power of language and self-talk in shaping our thoughts, emotions, and experiences. It highlights focus. As you know, where your focus goes, your energy flows.

Many people unknowingly use language that focuses on what they don't want, inadvertently attracting more of those undesirable outcomes into their lives. The subconscious mind doesn't recognise the difference between what you want and what you don't want—it simply responds to the content of your thoughts and words.

For example, someone might say, "I don't want to be stressed." However, by focusing on the concept of stress, they inadvertently invite more stress into their lives. Instead, they could reframe their statement to focus on what they do want, such as, "I want to feel calm and relaxed."

Similarly, someone might say, "I don't want to fail." Again, this language emphasises the fear of failure rather than focusing on success. A more empowering statement would be "I will achieve my goals and succeed in my endeavours."

By shifting your language to focus on what you want rather than what you don't want, you align your thoughts and intentions with your desired outcomes. This positive framing helps to cultivate a mindset of abundance, possibility, and empowerment, increasing the likelihood of manifesting your goals and dreams.

This rule number eleven is a great reminder of the importance of conscious language and self-talk in creating the life you desire. By choosing your words carefully and focusing on what you want to attract into your life, you will harness the power of your thoughts and intentions to create positive change and fulfilment.

12. Don't yell, don't complain, and don't harm

This is probably my favourite quote ever from Benjamin Franklin: "I resolve to speak ill of no man whatever, [but] all the good I know of everybody."

I'm convinced that if you apply this one principle or rule for a fulfilled life, you're going to immediately increase your threshold for success and fulfilment.

Charles F Haanel said something similar: "Eliminate, therefore, any possible tendency to complain of conditions as they have been or as they are, because it rests with you to change them and make them what you would like them to be. ... Our future is entirely within our own control. It is not at the mercy of any capricious or uncertain external power."

Complaining and yelling are both expressions of negative emotions that can exacerbate the intensity of those emotions, leading to increased feelings of frustration, anger, or dissatisfaction. Research has shown that engaging in these behaviours or reactions actually amplifies the negative emotions we're experiencing, making us feel even worse about the situation.

When you complain, you focus your attention on what's wrong or lacking, reinforcing a victim mentality and fostering a sense of powerlessness. Similarly, yelling in anger or frustration only serves to escalate the situation, creating tension and discord in our relationships and surroundings.

Instead of succumbing to the urge to complain or yell, it's important to cultivate a mindset of positivity and personal accountability, especially personal accountability, because you are a creator. You are a creator of your circumstances and emotions. This involves reframing setbacks and challenges as opportunities for growth and learning rather than sources of frustration or despair.

By adopting a mindset of gratitude, curiosity, and self-awareness, you can navigate life's ups and downs with grace and resilience. Rather than blaming others or external circumstances for your problems, take ownership of your experiences and empower yourself to create positive change. Embracing humour, humility, and a willingness to learn from failure are key components of this mindset. Learning to laugh at yourself, treat setbacks with curiosity, and maintain a sense of optimism even in the face of adversity is essential for personal growth and fulfilment.

Take responsibility for your thoughts and actions, maintain a positive attitude, and keep moving forward with resilience, determination, and a smile on your face.

13. Make conscious decisions

You've probably heard the statistic that you make over 30,000 decisions every day.

But did you know that, several decades ago, researchers discovered that 90% of those decisions are subconscious? We already talked about it in this book. Your life is driven by a subconscious mind based on all the limiting beliefs, values, and behaviours we learned when we were young. We created the program. We are now, later in life, on autopilot, as you see almost 90% of the time.

That is to say that you don't even think about the decisions you are making.

Pause for a minute.

This means that 90% of your life is determined automatically by your subconscious.

The results you get ...

The experience you have ...

The outcomes you produce ...

How much money you make ...

It's your automatic instincts that are actually guiding your life. How you *instinctively* present yourself to others. How you respond to particular situations. How you *instinctively* respond to criticism. How you *instinctively* react to failure or setbacks. How you make decisions and daily choices. The list is around 30,000 decisions long.

The real secret to fulfilment is that if you can learn to retrain your habits, your instincts, and your mind and harness your mind so you lead consciously day-to-day, decide consciously at each moment, and make choices that are more beneficial to you ... and then you can change *everything* about your life.

The instincts you have now might be benefiting you ... or they might be holding you back from achieving your desired outcome and true potential. So how do you retrain your subconscious thoughts and start making conscious decisions?

Practice. As I mentioned, it is great to have a guide or coach, but the important part of this work happens by practising awareness, catching that one-minute decision-making moment and changing the pattern, meditating, using breathing techniques, and being present day-to-day.

Napoleon Hill said, "The subconscious mind [...] makes no distinction between constructive and destructive thought impulses. It works with the material we feed it, through our thought impulses. The subconscious mind will translate into reality a thought driven by fear just as readily as it will translate into reality a thought driven by courage, or faith."

Some of the practices my clients do daily are mindful meditations or breath work. You can find some meditations at the end of this book with direct links to guided visualisation or mindful meditations to help you bring awareness to your daily mind and harness the power of consciousness. Train your mind, rewire your brain, and live a better life.

Chapter 11

Judgement and Mindset Shift

Before I start, I would like to clarify that we are talking here about thinking patterns of ongoing judgement—judging others and ourselves does not serve us. I am not talking about the instinctive judgement of a dangerous situation. This type of judgement is something that happens automatically and we respond to danger in different ways. Some people run, some people fight, some freeze.

In this chapter, we are talking about unnecessary judgement. Imagine yourself sitting at a coffee shop in Europe—maybe in a small Italian town—and sipping your coffee while watching the crowd. Normally, people start to watch the passersby and judge them. *This person is too fat, too small, has bad clothes* or *this person looks better than me and can dress up better. I am useless. I will never belong here.* And so on.

This is the judgement that evokes emotions and creates sensations and feelings in our body. We feel better about ourselves or feel worse about ourselves.

Dr John Demartini teaches that when we place people on pedestals or put them down, we create imbalances in our perceptions and emotions that impact our brain function, energy levels, and overall wellbeing. The whole focus of energy goes to the emotional brain and amygdala, so we kind of become silly and less intellectual while judging.

When we place someone on a pedestal, we idealise them, attributing to them qualities and virtues that we perceive as superior to our own. This can lead to feelings of inadequacy or inferiority within ourselves as we compare our own perceived shortcomings to the perceived greatness of the individual on the pedestal. This imbalance in perception can trigger feelings of insecurity, unworthiness, and low self-esteem, diminishing our sense of self-worth and self-confidence.

Conversely, when we put someone down, we diminish their value or worth in our eyes, often as a means of elevating our own sense of superiority or self-importance. This judgmental attitude can stem from feelings of envy, resentment, or insecurity, as we seek to bolster our own ego by belittling others. However, this behaviour ultimately perpetuates a cycle of negativity and divisiveness, creating barriers to genuine connection and understanding.

In both cases, the act of judgement distorts our perception of reality, clouding our ability to see others—and ourselves—with clarity and compassion. It creates energy blockages that inhibit the free flow of love, empathy, and understanding, leading to feelings of disconnection and isolation.

Dr Demartini emphasises the importance of cultivating a mindset of love, gratitude, and acceptance in overcoming the harmful effects of judgement. This involves recognising the inherent value and worth of every individual, regardless of their perceived strengths or weaknesses. By practising empathy and compassion towards ourselves and others, we can dissolve the barriers of judgement and foster deeper connections based on mutual respect and understanding.

In essence, Dr Demartini's teachings on judgement remind us of the power of perception in shaping our thoughts, emotions, and interactions with others. By releasing judgement and embracing a mindset of love and acceptance, we can elevate our consciousness, expand our capacity for connection, and cultivate greater harmony and fulfilment in our lives.

"It's absolutely easy to say but harder to practise," my clients said. I don't agree. I always say this is the easiest task you have in life. Why is that?

Well, all you need to do is to pause. Take a deep breath anytime you feel a bit of resistance or negative feelings or when you find yourself going to judgement in your mind. Just pause, nothing else. And then? You will see how ridiculous your thoughts want to be, but by pausing, you are breaking the old habits and old patterns of thinking and feeling, so great job! Does this sound hard? To me, not anymore, because I tried it a hundred times and stopped judging. So, your task is to start now and practise anytime you can. If you forget, don't blame yourself, and don't feel guilty or angry. Just go with life and bring conscious focus to your judgemental thoughts anytime you can. It will happen more often with time and later on, one day, you will realise I was right and you are not doing it anymore.

Microhabits—techniques for change

The brain is able to create neural connections when something new is concluded. In the journey of personal growth and transformation, the concept of microhabits plays a crucial role in rewiring the brain and creating lasting behavioural change. These small, incremental actions, when consistently practised, have the power to forge new neural pathways and solidify positive habits that lead to success and fulfilment.

Consider the story of Sarah, who decided to incorporate a morning routine of running and meditation into her daily life. Determined to start her day on the right foot, she committed to waking up at 5 am and heading straight to the beach, where she would run and meditate in the beautiful surroundings and watch the sunrise. Initially, Sarah felt motivated and energised by her new routine, but there were days when she struggled to find the motivation to lace up her shoes and hit the beach.

On those challenging days, Sarah faced a critical decision: to give in to the temptation of skipping her morning routine or to honour her commitment to herself and persevere despite the lack of motivation. She recognised that skipping days would only lead to a downward spiral of guilt, self-doubt, and regression to old habits. Also, not keeping promises to yourself truly damages your self-esteem. So, even on days when she didn't feel like it, Sarah made a conscious effort to show up at the beach, and even if she couldn't muster the energy to run, she would put on her trainers, take a walk, and meditate.

By taking these small steps, Sarah ensured that she didn't break the momentum of her new habit. Rain or shine, she showed up for herself, honouring her commitment and reinforcing the neural connections associated with her morning routine. Over time, what started as a conscious effort became second nature to Sarah as her new habit became deeply ingrained in her daily life and subconscious behavioural pattern.

Sarah's story illustrates the power of microhabits in creating lasting change. By breaking down her desired behaviour into small, manageable actions and committing to consistent practice, she was able to overcome obstacles and build resilience during the challenging mornings. Each small victory reinforced her confidence and self-esteem, paving the way for continued growth and progress.

If you are trying to break old patterns and integrate a new pattern or habit into your life, it's essential to celebrate every small win and remain steadfast in your commitment to personal growth. With patience, persistence, and the power of microhabits, you can transform your life one small step at a time. So, any ideas?

What is the next behavioural pattern you would like to change?

I have another great one for you.

This story illustrates the power of implementing a conscious pause to break a habitual behaviour pattern. Meet David, a client who had developed a routine of drinking wine or spirits with every dinner, a habit he was keen to change to improve his health and wellbeing.

David recognised that his evening ritual of pouring himself a drink had become automatic, almost instinctual, a behaviour deeply ingrained in his daily routine. It was just a habit; he did not need to do it. However, he also understood the negative impact this habit was having on his health and his ability to achieve his goals. The power of change starts with understanding what you sacrifice by continuing the old habit. What is the pain you are causing yourself and others now, or what will be the future pain and issues you will cause if you continue the old habit?

Determined to break free from his reliance on alcohol, David decided to introduce a simple yet powerful practice into his evening routine—a conscious pause. When his old habit kicked in and he was automatically reaching out for the bottle, David began by pausing. David took a moment to pause and centre himself. With the bottle of wine in hand, he closed his eyes and took a deep, intentional breath through his nose, allowing the aroma to fill his senses. He then released a long, audible exhale through his mouth, repeating this process three times, each breath deeper and more deliberate than the last.

In those moments of pause, David found clarity and perspective. He asked himself a simple yet profound question: "Do I still need it, or is it just an old habit?" Through this conscious inquiry, David confronted his habitual behaviour and reevaluated his choices.

More often than not, David's answer was no. The act of pausing and consciously breathing allowed him to tap into his inner wisdom and recognise that he didn't need alcohol to enjoy his meal or relax after a long day. Instead, he found satisfaction and fulfilment in savouring his non-alcoholic beverage and fully engaging in the present moment. Also, what he noticed he enjoyed the dinner conversation much more, he was more present and also listened deeply. He felt great and he became a conscious observer and learnt even more from each moment of clarity. His reward was feeling great and cultivating a state of joy every day. Now when he goes out to drink with his friends, his new habitual reaction is to say, "I'm driving, guys; I won't drink." This change was because he experienced the other side effects of not drinking in a very conscious way.

Over time, David's practice of implementing a conscious pause became second nature to him. He no longer felt the urge to reach for the bottle out of habit; instead, he embraced the opportunity to pause, reflect, and consciously choose the path that aligned with his health and wellbeing goals. He was happy he didn't feed his body with the poison. This decision helped improve his confidence and self-esteem, too.

David's story demonstrates the transformative power of introducing mindful practices into our daily routines. By incorporating a simple yet intentional pause into his evening ritual, he was able to break free from a deeply ingrained habit and create space for positive change and growth in his life.

Most people see this as very hard. On the other hand, it is never hard when you make a decision. I would love to point out this as the most important part of the change. A lot of people going through life saying: "I wish I wasn't drinking! I wish I wasn't that angry!" But the truth is that this is not their real authentic wish. These are only words, almost empty words. I know it may sound harsh. But I know it not only from my own experience but also from the experience of thousands of my clients.

So let's clarify. If you feel like you are in a vicious cycle and every time you try to change something you come back to the old habit again and again, feeling guilty and angry about yourself and feeling like you failed so many times becomes a nightmare. Well, there are a few important steps before you decide to change your habit again:

1. A decision needs to be made. Be aware of authenticity and internal decisions. That means you need to decide whether you are sure you want to stop drinking. Are you sure you want to stop or change whatever you are doing? I mean truly sure? Is that true? Can you see yourself without this old habit? Try to visualise how you will look, feel, do, and hear around you without the old habit!

2. Blockages need to be brought into awareness and unlocked. Find what you are afraid of. What are your worries about letting go of this old habit? One of my clients wants to change his habit of perfectionism and working hard to exhaustion, but on the other hand, he says, "But it brought me this far. What if I let go of everything and everything is worse? Won't my business stop growing, my house be dirty, and so on?"

Well, I ask, "And what if this doesn't happen?" and we continue coaching through these blockages. What if the opposite is true? And what if you only arrive here with this old habit and that's why you feel stuck and exhausted? What if, now, the next chapter of your life's new habit needs to be integrated to move you forward? We can create so many what-ifs. But what-ifs are not reality—they are assumptions about the future, so I challenge the client to test it and see for ourselves. This points to their limited subconscious thinking patterns and patterns of worries about the future. So we need to remove those.

3. The decision needs to be emotional. If your decision about change is not emotionally and energetically charged, it's pretty useless to try to implement sustainable change. You need to be aware of the pain of doing your life the old way. What will be the result if you continue the old way? What else could happen if you continue? How do you feel about that picture of the future? What about the positive vision of who you will become with the new habit? How are you feeling about yourself? How do others raise you up on their platforms and lives? How do you manage life and how will your relationships and health improve? How are you feeling about that? So now, you have visual and emotional connections attached to the habit.

4. You must have commitment and accountability. Now you have decided to keep going with your new habit. How do you keep yourself accountable? How committed are you, on a scale of 1 (not committed) to 10 (supercharged to change; nothing can stop me)? Who do you need to help you? Talk to your family and tell them what will help you. Talk to your coach and ask them for help.

5. Celebrate! When you implement your new habit, drop into your body and feel the sensations and feelings. How does your new habit make you feel today? How are you feeling about yourself? Grateful for your inner power and drive? Say thank you to yourself and others. Celebrate and reward yourself, but please don't reward yourself with a cheat meal or glass of wine when you are trying to stop drinking or eating junk food. That is contradicting and destroying your new habit change. Be grateful for small wins. Help someone else to do the same with you. Celebrate internally. Acknowledge yourself.

Microhabits consist of these steps in negative subconscious patterns:

1. Stimulus—which, in our case, can be feeling tired after work and wanting to recharge. Wanting to feel a release from the stress and worries of day-to-day life
2. Routine—this can be having a glass of wine or junk food when tired
3. Reward—the feeling of release and relaxation

Microhabits consist of these steps in positive conscious patterns when we try to rewire our brains:

1. Stimulus—which, in our case, can be feeling tired after work and wanting to recharge. Wanting to feel a release from the stress and worries of day-to-day life
2. Routine—this can start with a pause and three slow, deep breaths
3. Reward—the feeling of release and relaxation
4. Celebration—taking a glass of water with lemon and celebrating the feeling of release without alcohol or any junk food. Acknowledging yourself consciously and witnessing the proof you can do it. Your self-esteem will increase and dopamine or other happy hormones will be released. You will have new energy for doing even more, maybe exercise or walking, so every time you will feel more and more recharged

To me, this is probably the simplest way to describe small changes and their ripple effect on your life.

Chapter 12

The CEB Method in Practice

Developing and integrating the **CEB (conscious, emotional, and behavioural)** method was a turning point in my work with clients—and in my own life. I designed this method not as a quick fix but as a comprehensive, transformative process that addresses the emotional body, mindset, and behaviours to create a full identity shift. This shift is what truly changes a person's vibration, altering the way they attract experiences and how they respond to the world around them.

At the core of the CEB method lies the understanding that our outer reality mirrors our inner state. The results we see in life—whether in relationships, career, health, or wealth—are reflections of the thoughts we consistently think, the emotions we habitually feel, and the actions we repeatedly take. However, most people attempt to create change by focusing on actions alone. They hustle, push, and force results without addressing the root cause—**who they are being.**

The CEB method works by addressing this at the identity level first. When we change **who we are at our core,** our actions naturally shift. These new actions create different outcomes, and our external world begins to reflect this new state of being.

The process of neuro-identity shift

Imagine standing at a fork in the road. One path leads to repeating old patterns, staying stuck in the same emotional cycles and attracting similar results. The other path requires courage—a willingness to break free from past identities, self-doubt, and limiting beliefs. Taking a risk, stepping into the unknown. This is where the real work begins.

Through the CEB method, I guide clients to step onto the second path. We start by identifying the thoughts and emotional patterns that keep them in a loop. Often, they are unaware of how deeply ingrained these patterns are in their day-to-day actions until we shine a light on them. From this awareness, we begin to reshape their emotional blueprint.

A client I worked with, let's call her Sarah, came to me feeling stuck in every area of her life. Her business wasn't growing, her relationships were strained, and she felt exhausted—mentally, emotionally, and physically. Sarah believed she was doing all the right things—networking, marketing, and showing up consistently. But beneath the surface, she carried the subconscious belief that she wasn't worthy of success. Her energy radiated that belief, even if she didn't realise it. She was only seeing and attracting confirmation of this belief—identity.

Through our work, Sarah started by addressing the emotional body. Together, we uncovered past experiences that left her feeling unseen and unheard. This created patterns of overworking and overgiving, as she tried to prove her worth. I led her through emotional release techniques, deep reflective exercises, and meditation practices to shift this energy towards who she truly wants to be and how she wants to feel.

As Sarah's emotional body healed, her **vibration shifted.** She began to feel lighter, more confident, and grounded. Her thoughts followed suit—shifting from self-doubt to *I am capable and deserving.*

Without forcing it, her actions started to reflect this new identity. She stopped chasing clients and instead began attracting aligned opportunities. Within weeks, she signed three major contracts effortlessly—relationships she had been trying to cultivate for months suddenly materialised.

This wasn't a coincidence. It was a result of her **identity shift.**

Understanding the emotional body

The emotional body is often the most neglected part of personal development, but it holds immense power. Our emotions act as signals, revealing where we are aligned or misaligned with our true selves. When unresolved emotions accumulate, they create blocks in the energy system, manifesting as stress, procrastination, or even physical ailments.

In the CEB method, we acknowledge emotions not as enemies but as **teachers.** Instead of suppressing anger, fear, or sadness, we meet them with curiosity. By processing these emotions, the energy they hold is released, and we free ourselves from repeating those patterns. This process is expressed through the biological body—with less fear, stress, doubt, and anxiety, the levels of neurotransmitters that don't serve us, such as cortisol and adrenal hormones, start decreasing. So, we start the process of healing and shifting our energetic body expressed in frequency.

Another client, **James,** struggled with leadership in his company. He had the skills and experience, but his team didn't respect him, and he constantly felt like he had to prove himself. After diving deeper, we discovered that James had unresolved feelings of rejection from his childhood. This created a subconscious pattern of needing external validation.

As James worked through these emotions, his confidence grew. His body language shifted, and his communication became clearer and more assertive. His team responded to this new energy—respect and cooperation naturally followed. This had a positive impact on clients and employee retention.

Behavior follows identity

Most of us try to change behaviours first—pushing ourselves to build habits, exercise more, or be more productive, creating New Year's resolutions and things we want to "do to become". But the truth is that behavioural change that isn't rooted in **identity work** rarely sticks. When we try to force new actions while still identifying as the same person, we sabotage ourselves.

For example, if you see yourself as someone who struggles with money, you can try budgeting or cutting expenses, but the underlying identity of "I'm bad with money" will override those actions. Eventually, you'll return to old patterns.

The CEB method addresses this disconnect by shifting identity first. When you start identifying as someone who is financially responsible and abundant, **the actions of budgeting, saving, and investing become natural extensions of who you are.**

Creating a new vibration

Everything in the universe operates at a frequency, and humans are no different. When we carry low-vibration emotions like guilt, shame, or fear, we attract experiences that match that frequency. The CEB method works to elevate this vibration by aligning thoughts, emotions, and behaviours with higher states like **joy, gratitude, and love.**

One of the most profound examples of this was with a client, **Lena,** who wanted to attract a partner but continuously found herself in relationships that mirrored her insecurities. Through our work, she uncovered a core belief that she wasn't lovable.

By shifting her identity to someone who valued and cherished herself, Lena's energy transformed. Within months, she met someone who reflected that new state back to her.

The ripple effect of transformation

Identity shifts don't just change one area of life—they create ripples across all areas. As clients shift internally, they report breakthroughs in business, deeper personal relationships, improved health, and overall life satisfaction.

The CEB method isn't just about achieving goals—it's about becoming the person who naturally creates those goals.

When you shift your identity, everything else follows.

Resources, Inspirations, and a Thank You to My Teachers and Mentors

Thank you to all my mentors and the coaches I am working and collaborating with, and a special thank you to all the teachers, mentors and life influencers:

My parents and my family,

My husband

Dr Joe Dispenza,

The Coaching Institute,

Enterprise Agility University,

Chris Jackson,

PK Savy,

Joe Pane,

Tony Robbins,

Fara Curlewis,

Dan Brulé,

Ray Behan,

Michael Singer.

Resources

Maslow's Hierarchy of Needs:

en.wikipedia.org/wiki/Maslow's_hierarchy_of_needs

Emotional Intelligence:

Daniel Goleman, *Working with Emotional Intelligence*, Bloomsbury Pub Ltd, 1999.

Meditation Practices

- Claim free meditation here:

https://thementoringeffect.com/disconnect-to-reconnect/

- Transformation with meditation in 5 days mini course:

https://leadership-university.mykajabi.com/offers/k2NyHDKR/checkout

- Free meditations for listening from YouTube®:

https://youtu.be/4IakGfKUcT0?si=xmArBAPpJswzIm0L

https://youtu.be/j8xUA7s_OVM?si=dPIx6OJRKL8gMk7h

https://thementoringeffect.com/resources/

Podcasts

Alex's podcasts can be found on iTunes® and Spotify®:
- Conscious Leadership with Alex podcast
- Limitless Soul podcast

Our limitless mind -

to learn more about our limitless mind follow our new program:

https://thementoringeffect.com/limitless-mind-foundation/

and

https://thementoringeffect.com/limitless-mind/

www.ingramcontent.com/pod-product-compliance
Lightning Source LLC
Chambersburg PA
CBHW070659120526
44590CB00013BA/1031